kitchen harvest

kitchen
harvest

GROWING ORGANIC FRUIT, VEGETABLES AND HERBS IN CONTAINERS

SUSAN BERRY

photographs by
STEVEN WOOSTER

illustrations by
MADELEINE DAVID

FRANCES LINCOLN

*In memory of my grandmother, Alice Lee Jones, a good gardener and a great cook,
and her two daughters: my mother, Patti, and my aunt, Mary.*

Frances Lincoln Limited
4 Torriano Mews
Torriano Avenue
London NW5 2RZ
www.franceslincoln.com

KITCHEN HARVEST

First Frances Lincoln edition 2002
First paperback edition 2003

British Library Cataloguing-in-Publication data
A catalogue record for this book is available from the British Library

ISBN 0 7112 1896 Hardback
ISBN 0 7112 2135 9 Paperback

A Berry Book
47 Crewys Road
Childs Hill
London NW2 2AU

Designed by Anne Wilson

Printed in Singapore

4 6 8 9 7 5

contents

PLANNING THE GARDEN

Just a few of the many edible plants you can grow on a small patio. The selection here includes two types of bean, chard, cabbages, courgettes, rocket and beetroot, as well as raspberries and blueberries.

There is a surprisingly wide range of edible plants that you can grow successfully in containers, but almost all need a sunny position. If you are growing edible plants in containers for the first time, it is best to concentrate your energies on those that are relatively easy to grow. Herbs are ideal as they will grow well in even the smallest containers, and a windowsill will suffice for a good range of different culinary herbs, such as parsley, chives, sage, thyme and basil. Among the easier vegetables are most salad greens, radishes, potatoes, courgettes, tomatoes and French and runner beans. Of the fruit, strawberries usually do well in containers, as do currants. Most tree fruit are more demanding, but it is still enjoyable to try one or two in pots.

Not all edible plants are hardy, and those that are tender require more care if you are growing them in a cold climate. You will need to sow the seeds indoors early so that the plants get the longest possible time for ripening, and, if you are growing tender fruit trees, for example, you may need to overwinter them indoors in very cold weather or wrap the containers in bubblewrap to provide protection against light frosts.

If you are attracted to the idea of growing produce in containers, you probably do not have a great deal of space. When deciding what to grow, you need to work out how many containers you can position in a reasonably sunny place and then plan what you plant accordingly. There is no point in raising vast quantities of seedlings if there is no space to plant them out!

SMART SPACE Grow climbing varieties, whenever you can, as they take up vertical, as opposed to horizontal, space. Remember, though, that if you grow a

OPPOSITE It is worth looking out for unusual varieties, such as cucumber 'Lockies Perfection' (top) and shallot onion 'Long Red Florence' (bottom), as experimenting is half the fun of growing edible plants in containers.

grape vine it will cast shade under the foliage, which will preclude growing most vegetables underneath its canopy, so site this away from your growing space. Tomatoes are clearly among the best container-grown crops, as indeed are outdoor cucumbers. You can even grow tomatoes, such as 'Tumbler', in hanging baskets if you wish. You can also use hanging baskets for lettuces, strawberries, herbs, and even rocket and radishes. But remember that they dry out very quickly, so copious and frequent watering will be required in hot weather. Seaweed meal moisture retainer will help to water loss.

It is vital to make the best use of a small space, so ideally you need to plan successive sowings, re-using containers as you harvest the crops. You can interplant larger, later maturing crops with smaller, faster growing ones. For example, radishes are very fast growing and can be planted in and among slower growing plants, such as beans. You can plant some vegetables and fruit among flowering plants: grow strawberries with lettuces and pansies, for instance. If you lose a few edible plants in a container to pests or diseases, fill the container up with a smaller crop, or with flowers, rather than leaving the container half empty. Make or buy staging so that you can create a tier of containers.

WHAT TO GROW

You can grow pretty well any vegetable or fruit in a container, but the issue is not what you can grow, but what it is sensible or worthwhile to grow. The choice of vegetables, fruit and herbs in this book has been determined by what tastes so good that only a small quantity will be a sufficient delight to eat and maybe cook. There is little point in growing staple crops that are relatively inexpensive to buy. Look for interesting varieties, such as striped tomatoes, yellow carrots or unusually shaped chillies (see individual entries for specific suggestions), since half the fun of growing edible plants in containers is to show off your crop.

ORGANIC METHODS

One of the principal reasons organic methods were replaced by chemicals was the sheer scale of the problem in commercial growing of trying to prevent pests and diseases from ravaging the crop. Organic gardening demands rather more personal attention than the chemical

approach of blast-everything-first. However, precisely because you have a tiny garden growing under your nose you will see problems early on and can deal with them quickly and efficiently, if necessary by hand. If your container garden is on a balcony you will not, happily, be troubled by slugs and snails (unless a careless bird drops one by mistake!). However, if you have a ground-level terrace or patio, you will have to watch out for them (see pages 28–9).

To feed your plants, you can now buy a good range of organic fertilizers (see page 140), if necessary by mail order or via the internet, or you can use well-rotted manure or home-made compost.

choosing varieties

When you grow edible plants in containers, you enter the food-farming world in microcosm, and you learn some interesting lessons as a consequence. In recent years there has been an emphasis on breeding vegetables and fruit that are commercially useful, and reserach has been directed towards maximizing profit for the farmer. As your own producer of limited supplies of food, you are probably more interested in flavour than yield, and your choice of variety should be made with this in mind. In the days before the profit motive became such an issue, this principle applied to many of the smaller commercial growers, too.

You will find, therefore, that many of the old varieties give you the intensity of flavour you desire. That being said, however, one of the benefits of modern breeding has been to create varieties that are more disease or pest resistant. Only when you have lost your entire, much-valued crop of one particular plant do you realize that this is a major issue!

By far the most important aspect of choosing varieties for containers is the amount of space that the plants take up and it is therefore well worth while looking for dwarf varieties that will give you a good yield while taking up much less room. Even the considerations of space, though, should not stop you from experimenting with a range of varieties. Individual vegetable, fruit and herb entries in this book offer suggestions as to what you might best grow.

A selection of seeds, demonstrating the many different forms and sizes in which they come. Clockwise, from top left, these are: peas, beans, nasturtium, haricot beans, garlic, radishes, courgettes and beetroot.

If you grow naturally pollinated varieties, rather than F1 hybrids, you can save the seed of your own plants for next year's crop. With F1 hybrids, which have been purpose bred, the progeny will either not breed true to type or may be completely sterile. If you want to grow open-pollinated varieties, you will probably need to purchase seed by mail order from a specialist supplier (see page 142). One such potato grower in Scotland maintains 400 varieties of potato, for example. While it is interesting, too, to obtain catalogues from foreign seed merchants, bear in mind that they have developed cultivars best suited to the local climate.

If a particular variety you have grown has pleased you and it is not an F1 hybrid, then consider letting a few plants ripen to seed and saving it. Since many plants tend to cross-pollinate, if you want to keep the seed true to type, you need to put a paper bag over the flowerhead and hand-pollinate it yourself by brushing the pollen from one flower onto the reproductive parts of another.

SAVING SEED

If the seeds are encased in pods, it is best to allow these to dry on the plant naturally to ensure the seed is fully ripe. Then transfer them to paper bags and take them indoors to a warm, dry spot, having labelled each one with the variety name and date of harvest. After that, keep them in a cool, dark place until needed. Some seed remains viable for years, but others will be unusable after a year so it is best, generally, to use the seed sooner rather than later.

choosing containers

You can grow edible plants in any container, as long as it is deep enough to allow room for the roots to spread, and contains enough growing medium for the take-up of nutrients. What the latter does not contain in the way of nutrients at the outset, or loses over the growing period, can be supplemented with various types of organic feed.

However, if you are growing edible plants in a small space, a secondary objective is to ensure that you create an aesthetically pleasing display. Since the plants themselves are not grown primarily for their beauty (although some edible plants are ornamental as well as functional), you can make up for this by choosing handsome containers or, at the very least, trying to impose some uniformity and order on the whole display.

For many years organic gardening has, quite rightly, involved a strong element of recyling, but you can recycle without turning your balcony or terrace into a junkyard. By all means re-use old tins but paint them in subtle colours. Old terracotta pots have immense appeal, thanks to the particularly attractive faded colour that they acquire in time and the irregular shapes that they present if hand-thrown. You can turn a brand new, offensively bright ginger, machine-made terracotta pot into something more subtle by 'antiquing' it: simply paint yoghourt (any old out-of-date pots will do) onto the pot with a brush, and leave it to dry. The bacteria will encourage the formation of algae, and the pot will rapidly acquire a much classier personality!

If you decide to recycle aluminium pots (such as old buckets or wash-tubs), you must make drainage holes in the base first. You can do this with a bradawl and brute force, or you can use a power drill with a metal bit, which is fast but unpleasantly noisy. Drill at least half a dozen large holes for a container with a base 30cm (12in) across and more, pro rata, for a bigger one. Don't forget to scrub out all old pots before using them in order to get rid of any potentially harmful contents. Equally, recycled pots from the previous season's plants must all be scrubbed out to prevent viruses and other disease being passed on.

If you vary the sizes and shapes of the containers, you will be able to group any display more effectively and make better use of the available space. If you have a very tall container, such as an old chimney pot (ideal for deep-rooting vegetables like potatoes or leeks that need earthing up), you can also use it for smaller plants, too. Simply fill most of it with rubble and then top up the last 25cm (10in) or so of the container with compost, the depth depending on what you want to grow.

OPPOSITE Even a relatively small container, such as an old bucket, will be large enough to produce a good crop of runner or French beans.

BELOW LEFT Recycled metal pots, including a washtub, buckets, a watering can, a coal scuttle and a colander, are all suitable containers.

BELOW RIGHT Various sizes and shapes of terracotta pot, including a small window box and a special strawberry planter.

To maximize the use of space, you can grow edible plants in hanging baskets. Strawberries are a particularly good choice, as are lettuces, rocket, radishes and many different herbs, particularly the bushy, low-growing ones such as thyme, marjoram and parsley. Nasturtiums, of which both the flowers and seeds are edible, also do very well in hanging baskets, although they are susceptible to blackfly.

CONTAINER SIZE It is important when growing edible plants to ensure that the container holds enough growing medium for the plant to develop successfully. To this end, the depth of the container is as important as the diameter, particularly for root crops, plants that need earthing up and fruit trees. Small, fast-growing plants can be grown in relatively small containers (mustard and cress, some salad crops, radishes and herbs can be grown in 20cm/8in diameter pots), but generally the minimum size is 25cm (10in) in diameter with a similar depth. Root vegetables, such as potatoes, do best in much deeper containers (around 45cm/18in deep at least) to ensure the roots have room to grow to their full length.

planting medium

The medium in which you grow your edible plants will determine how well they grow, so it is important to do your research carefully, if you want to ensure that there is something to pick at the end of all the hard work of sowing, watering and feeding. The general kind of multi-purpose compost provided by garden centres is not organic so if you want to ensure your plants are fully organic, buy your compost from a specialist supplier (or look for compost that has been approved by an appropriate organization) or make up your own planting medium (see page 140). There are a number of organic products that form the bulky base, such as coir (coconut fibre) and wood products, to which grit, potash and lime are added in varying quantities, according to the formulation required. The multi-purpose formulation is adequate for most vegetables, fruit and herbs as most vegetables and fruit grow well in soil that has an average level of acidity. This is soil with a pH rating (by which the level of acidity/alkalinity is graded) of 5.5–7. A lower pH indicates a higher acidity, a higher pH higher alkalinity.

However, brassicas like a more alkaline soil, and need a pH of around 7, so you may need to add a little lime to the compost. You can buy this in bags, and you will need to add only a tablespoonful to the average 30cm (12in) diameter container. Blueberries like very acid soil, and you will have to use an ericaceous (acid) compost for them rather than a standard mix. Equally, you can make your own mix more acid by adding recycled peat. Remember that in hard-water areas watering with tap water can reduce the level of acidity, and if you are growing plants that prefer acid conditions, it may be best to collect rainwater in a barrel.

PLANT PREFERENCES

If you are in doubt as to the pH level of your potting medium you can test it with an over-the-counter testing kit, in which a small sample of the medium is mixed with liquid in a test tube. This liquid turns colour and you can read off the pH levels by comparing colours on the accompanying chart. Corrections to the acidity levels can be made by adding lime or spent mushroom compost to increase the alkalinity while leafmould or well-rotted organic material will increase the acidity.

TESTING ACIDITY LEVELS

Bear in mind that any planting medium loses its nutrients after a short time – as they are leached out through watering and rainfall – so it is best to buy, or make it, in smallish quantities rather than to keep bags for months by which time most of the nutrients will have disappeared.

POTTING MEDIUM LONGEVITY

BASIC CULTIVATION

equipment

When you start to produce crops in containers the first thing you will need is the wherewithal to do so. This does not amount to a lot: enough containers of different sizes, a small trowel and fork, a few pencils to act as dibbers, a watering can (and possibly a hose if you have a large patio or terrace), a small 900ml (1½pt) sprayer, and seed trays and blocks, as well as a propagator if you want to grow more exotic vegetables. If you are going to make your own compost, you will need a container with a capacity of at least 1 cu m (1 cu yd) to generate sufficient heat to

You will need a small selection of basic equipment and a few tools. Essential items are a watering can and hand-held sprayer, trowel and fork, secateurs, pruning saw, scissors and a garden knife, as well as garden wire and string.

accelerate the rotting process. It should also have a lid to keep in the warmth. If you have enough room, it is also a good idea to have a barrel to collect rainwater, as some plants are sensitive to the lime content in tap water in hard-water areas.

To extend your crop and keep off slugs and snails, cloches (even improvised ones made from cut-down clear-plastic bottles) are useful. When using canes, put a stopper on the end; more eye accidents occur when gardening than at any other time. Do not forget plastic labels and an indelible pen. If you do not label what you sow, you will fall into the embarrassing trap of not being able to remember what was sown when and where. I made the mistake of thinking my young cosmos plants were actually tomato plants until a kind, and more knowledgeable, friend pointed this out! Many young seedlings (before they develop their true leaves and colours) look deceptively similar.

In addition to the hardware, you will need a plentiful supply of organic potting medium, some multi-purpose organic fertilizer or the various different ingredients of fertilizer if you wish to try to mix your own (see page 140).

Some kind of work surface with a cupboard underneath is really useful, if only to save time clearing things away, but a couple of large storage boxes that can be pushed under a worktop or table, which you can use for seed sowing or potting up, will serve the purpose. To grow seedlings well indoors you need a light area, such as a wide shelf, away from direct sunlight.

sowing and planting

If you want some of the more unusual varieties mentioned in this book, you will need to obtain the seed from specialist growers (see Suppliers on page 142). Do not buy too much, as seed does not keep well after a season or two at most, and it is much better to obtain fresh supplies as and when you need them. These days, you get far fewer seeds in a packet than you once used to, so there is not much danger you will have far too much for your purposes, but if you can persuade a friend to grow edible plants, you can seed-swap and share packets. You need very little in the way of equipment to sow seeds, but if you want to grow plants that originate from hotter climates than your own, you may have to invest in a heated propagator, because some seeds will not germinate below certain temperatures. For the bulk of commonly grown vegetables and herbs, you need little more than a few seed trays, small plastic pots or compartmentalized seed units. Making use of old margarine or yoghourt pots is a cheap and effective way to recycle plastic, provided you remember to punch a few drainage holes in the base of the pots first.

The seeds of different plants vary greatly in size (and in appearance, too), but it is primarily the size that affects the way the seed is sown. The seed is a small capsule with all the genetic growing information the plant requires. Once it is provided with favourable conditions – and bear in mind that what is favourable to one plant may be death to another! – the trigger to sprout into life will be given. These conditions are the optimum degree of warmth, moisture and light to which the particular organism has been programmed to respond. Your job is to give the seeds these conditions and then to make sure that they continue to apply. It is no good carefully sowing your seeds and then completely forgetting about them. If you put them on a hot windowsill where they can bake in the sun or let the compost dry out, or sluice them with so much water that they drown or turn mouldy, your initial outlay will have been in vain.

The basic requirements for seed sowing are:
- enough depth of compost for the roots to form (but do not waste compost by using too much)
- fine enough compost for small seeds and seedlings to be able to force their way through it (it may need to be sieved)
- the right amount of warmth, moisture and light for germination to begin (seed packets give temperatures and timing)
- to make sure that,once germination has begun, the same conditions apply until the seedlings are planted out in their final positions.

Not much equipment is needed for sowing seeds, apart from a range of suitable seed trays or pots, a sieve, a dibber, labels and an indelible pen or pencil. If you want to sow seeds of tender plants, you will find a special propagation unit helpful as well.

If you do not have good overhead light (the ideal situation for seedlings), make sure you turn the trays of seedlings every day to prevent them growing towards the light. If there is not enough natural light, the seedlings will become etiolated (weak and spindly). Find a lighter position, or invest in daylight bulbs.

DEPTH OF SOWING

Very fine seed is generally sown on the surface of the compost and a fine layer of compost then sieved over it. Otherwise, you can work to a rule of thumb of sowing at approximately twice the depth of the seed for how deep to sow, but seed packets always give appropriate instructions.

SEED SPACING

If you sow carefully, you can prevent seed going to waste. However, since not all seed germinates, you should allow for more than you need (by around 50 per cent). If you are lucky and all the seeds grow, you will have to thin the seedlings out to a spacing that will allow the plants to develop properly. This spacing is determined by how big you want the eventual plant to grow. The newly fashionable mini-vegetables are basically plants that are packed in together and harvested while they are very young. They are tender but not always full of flavour (as flavour often develops with maturity) and are expensive in the shops because twice the amount of seed is used for half the eventual crop. But for the home grower, and particularly the container-gardening home grower, they are useful, because packets of seed are not particularly expensive.

TRANSPLANTING

Most seeds are sown in seed trays and transplanted into their containers when they are large enough to handle (when two true leaves have formed). However, there are a few plants, such as radishes, that dislike being transplanted and these will need to be sown *in situ* (see relevant entries). To transplant seedlings, use a fine dibber (a pencil is just right) to remove the seedling from the tray, then pick it up gently by the leaves, not by the stem, which bruises easily. Make a hole in the new compost with the dibber and gently drop the seedling into it. Firm the compost carefully around the newly planted seedling.

HARDENING OFF

To produce early crops of plants you need to put the young plants outside as soon as any frosts are over. Get them acclimatized to outdoor conditions by putting them outside in the day and bringing them in at night, when temperatures drop, for about a week. If you put a mini-cloche (a cut-down bottle is ideal) over a pot, this will help to keep the plant warm (and free from pest and disease attack) while it is acclimatizing. It will also enable you to grow plants earlier than otherwise you might, thereby extending the season.

BASIC PLANTING

When planting up large containers, remember to crock the pot (cover the drainage hole with pebbles or broken shards of pot) to make sure that the holes do not block up with compost and prevent free drainage. Always water plants in well and keep them well-watered while they are acclimatizing to their new home. Choose a container size that is suitable for the growth habit of the plant in question (see individual entries for suggestions on sizes). Fruit trees generally need a container that is 8cm (3in) larger than the root ball of the tree.

Various seedlings and young plants at different stages of growth. It pays to sow seed successively so that you do not harvest all your plants at once.

feeding

Many edible plants are surprisingly accommodating and will produce some kind of crop with very little help from you. But if you want the best tasting plants, you will need to feed them the right type of nutrients at the right time in roughly the right quantities. Each vegetable, or fruit, has quite specific demands for certain kinds of nutrients at certain times, since specific nutrients are needed at different stages of growth, such as for leaf, flower or fruit formation. For example, nitrogen produces leafy growth, and potash aids the production of fruit. While you can make up your own fertilizers in appropriate proportions, it is easier and quicker to buy ready-made ones.

Feeding too frequently with over-rich chemical-based fertilizers makes crops grow larger but they become tasteless in the process, so the secret is to find a good source of organic fertilizer that does the job effectively, without overdoing it. You can use home-made compost as a useful mulch and also as a supplementary feed, since it many not necessarily contain pecisely the nutrients required.

MAKING COMPOST

If you have room to do so, making your own compost is both useful and satisfying. You can buy a purpose-made compost bin with removable slats that will enable you to draw off the compost when it is ready. All you need to do is to store your vegetable and fruit peelings, together with tea leaves, coffee grounds and eggshells (but no cooked food) together with any plant waste (but not diseased plants or perennial weeds). If you can layer the ingredients with small amounts of shredded paper or straw, so much the better. When sufficient heat generates in the bin, bacteria will get to work rotting down the waste into a mixture rich in nitrogen. A small amount of compost activator applied to the heap as the layers build up will help to keep it all moving. You will need to keep the top covered to prevent the heap from becoming waterlogged, although it is a good idea to moisten the heap periodically so that the contents are not bone dry either. After about six months you should have usable compost from it.

Plant foods or fertilizers can be applied either in the form of pellets or granules, or watered direct onto the soil or onto the leaves (foliar feeds). The take-up rate of each of these forms of feed varies, the foliar feeds being the fastest, so they are most useful for providing a quick plant pick-me-up. However, they are not seen as being part of best organic practice in which the growing conditions should be improved first.

There are a number of good organic plant feeds available. One of the best is a mixture made from any rich organic matter, such as animal manure (enclosed in a muslin bag), steeped in water for 10 days or so. The nutrients in the organic matter will disperse into the water, providing you with a useful feed you can water onto the plants when needed. Dilute it to the colour of weak tea before applying it to the plants.

The potting compost used for planting up will last the plants for an average of six weeks, but after that you will need to provide supplementary feeding. This becomes even more important for fruiting plants (including tomatoes, aubergines and peppers), which need more copious feeding once the fruit starts to form. Generally, you will need to feed these plants every three to four weeks. Each plant entry explains approximately how often to feed the plants and with what.

watering

If you grow any plants in containers watering is a major priority. It is especially important to ensure that edible plants receive regular, generous quantities of water. If you are going to grow them on a balcony or roof terrace, it will pay you to organize a tap nearby – otherwise you may find yourself increasingly reluctant to water your plants.

Not only does regular, plentiful watering help the plants to grow to their full size and develop more succulent leaves and fruits, it will also help to prevent pests and diseases. Plants subjected to stress (and irregular watering is a major cause of this) are much less strong. Failure to water on a regular basis will lead to stunted growth, and over-watering to compensate does not help – it simply adds to the stress!

Courgettes are easy to grow and prolific, making excellent use of limited container space. They enjoy a deep, rich growing medium. Eat the surplus male flowers as well as the fruits.

To give you some idea of the amount of water required, a large barrel, fully planted, would lose up to 6 litres (1.3 gallons) of water a day in hot weather. Make sure when you water that you do more than simply wet the top surface of the soil. Fill your pots with compost to roughly 2.5cm (1in) from the rim, then, when you water fully grown plants, fill the container with water to the rim. Any surplus will simply drain away.

Seedlings are particularly susceptible to drought and will need regular watering from a watering can with a fine rose. Grouping plants together helps to cut down on potential moisture loss through transpiration and makes watering easier. Moisture-retaining seaweed meal can also be used to improve the water-holding capacity of the growing medium. A small handful, mixed in with the growing medium, will be sufficient.

WATERING EQUIPMENT AND DEVICES

All you need is a watering can with a fine rose attachment. Different styles of watering can are available, but the traditional galvanized metal watering cans (now being reproduced in smart gardening shops) are perfectly serviceable and look a lot more attractive than plastic ones.

If you have a roof terrace, balcony or patio you can install a drip watering system that does the job for you by delivering the water directly to the plants via linked tubing with tiny nozzles. However, the nozzles do tend to clog up with growing medium, and it is quite hard to disguise the tubing effectively, so unless you are away from home often, it is probably better to make the effort to hand-water your plants.

To help gauge water quantities, you can buy small moisture-reading sticks. You insert these into the compost, and they change colour when the growing medium starts to dry out. However, edible plants rely on generous amounts of water, so this so-called early warning system may deliver a warning that is a bit on the late side.

WHEN TO WATER

Always water in the early morning or evening on sunny days. The combination of water and sunlight can scorch the leaves, leaving unsightly brown patches and spoiling the crop on leafy vegetables.

supporting and protecting plants

If you are growing climbing or vining plants, you will need to provide an adequate support system for them, which will be determined by the way in which the plant climbs. Individual entries for vegetables and fruit include suggestions as to the type of support systems to use.

For climbing plants, such as runner beans, and for tomatoes, peppers and aubergines, which can be heavy when fully laden with a crop, a stout, well-anchored support system is essential. Other plants that do not climb but that have delicate or floppy stems may also benefit from some support. For dwarf varieties of peas and beans, for example, a simple system of short lengths of brushwood, inserted a few inches deep into the container close to the stem of the plant, will be all that is needed. For taller varieties, angled poles, tied together at the top to form a a wigwam shape, are ideal. Alternatively, grow the beans up trellis or on strings attached to a horizontal support roughly 2m (6ft) off the ground.

BELOW Cucumbers (left) need to be tied to a stout support, such as a cane. Floppy basil leaves (centre) can be contained with a few brushwood twigs. In summer fruit, such as redcurrants (right), will need to be netted to prevent birds from taking the crop.

Fast-growing plants requiring support, such as cucumbers and tomatoes, will need a strong cane or canes inserted at the time of planting and then a system of horizontal wires at 15cm (6in) intervals onto which the lateral shoots can be trained as the plant grows. A grape vine will need the sturdiest support system (see page 108), to which the new shoots will need to be tied in, because a fully laden vine at harvest time can become remarkably heavy. A supporting pergola is ideal and offers the bonus on a patio or balcony of a shaded area under the foliage on hot summer days.

In addition to providing growing suppport, you will need to give your plants some protection in colder weather. Low-growing vegetables and herbs can be protected with purpose-made or do-it-yourself see-through covers (known as cloches) of various description. A cut-down mineral water container, upturned over a pot, acts as an impromptu cloche and will also double up as protection for young seedlings from slug and snail damage. You can also buy small polytunnels, if you have sufficient space, or individual glass bell or barn cloches, or you can cover your crops with various see-through covers made from polythene, fleece or fine-net film. They are ideal not only for preventing damage from frosts but also for protecting young plants from flying insect pests. Remember, though, that insect pollination will not take place under these films so remove them from all except self-fertile plants just before they come into flower.

If you are growing tender fruit trees, you will need to consider winter protection for them in cold climates. You can either overwinter the plants indoors, if you have room, or you can wrap the containers in sacking or bubblewrap, which will afford the plants some protection.

Fine netting will be needed in summer to cover most fruit crops – otherwise birds will almost certainly consume them before you get the chance. Make sure the netting is fixed securely.

common pests and diseases

You are not alone in enjoying the flavour of organic produce. Pests of all descriptions may descend on them, eager to get their share of the produce. The good news is that container growing (particularly if you are gardening above ground level) cuts out most soil-borne pests, and good plant management, with appropriate feeding and watering, reduces the likelihood of disease. Watching your plants closely permits you to nip incipient attacks in the bud. To minimize diseases, make sure that all the pots you use are thoroughly cleaned before re-use. The following are the most common pests and diseases, although there is a much wider range that can attack your plants. See invididual entries for specific problems.

PESTS

aphids   These can be a particular nuisance. They suck the sap from young shoots and often transmit virus diseases in the process. Spray with insecticidal soap or derris as a last resort. Encouraging beneficial insects, such as ladybirds, will help to control them.

beetles and weevils   These tend to nibble plants, particularly radishes. Either cover the plants with fleece or spray with derris.

caterpillars   These attack the brassica family in particular. Use biological controls, net the crops or pick them off by hand. Underplanting cabbages with French marigolds helps to deter cabbage butterflies.

red spider mite   Mainly a glasshouse pest, this damages fruiting vegetables, especially in hot summers. Keep plants humid with frequent spraying. Biological controls can be used under glass.

scale insect   These can attack a wide range of plants. Spray with insecticidal soap.

slugs and snails   These attack the young shoots and leaves of a wide range of plants and will also eat tubers. Use nematodes or stand the pots in a moat of water.

whitefly   Loves brassicas. Plant French marigolds nearby or net the plants. Use biological controls in the greenhouse.

mildews This causes pale blotches on young leaves, yellow areas on older ones. Tips of leaves go grey and die back. Don't overcrowd young plants, particularly lettuces. Spray with sulphur at first signs of disease.

mosaic virus Various kinds attack different vegetables – cucumber, lettuce and tomatoes in particular. They cause mottling and puckering of leaf surface, and plants become stunted and may die. On tomatoes the fruit will be bronzed and blemished. The best defence is to buy virus-tested seeds. Destroy any affected plants immediately as the virus rapidly spreads.

DISEASES

magnesium deficiency Common on tomatoes, this causes leaves to yellow and drop. Caused by high potash feeds. Dress with Epsom salts.

calcium deficiency Blossom rots. Water regularly so that more calcium is taken up.

premature fruit drop Usually caused by irregular feeding and watering. Improve the feeding and watering regime.

fruit withering Affects cucumbers as a result of poor nutrition. Sometimes caused by rots.

premature flowering (bolting) Affects spinach, rocket, onions and oriental brassicas. Caused by inadequate watering in hot conditions.

DISORDERS

derris Use for aphids, beetles, caterpillars, red spider mite.

pyrethrum Use for caterpillars, whitefly, leafhoppers and aphids.

insecticidal soap Use for aphids, red spider mite and whitefly.

bordeaux mixture Use for blight.

sulphur Use for powdery mildew.

biological control Various forms exist. Check with organic associations and organic garden suppliers.

grease bands Use on fruit trees to deter pests.

ORGANIC CONTROLS

vegetables

roots · stems · leaves · fruiting vegetables · salad crops · other vegetables

potatoes
solanum tuberosum

Potatoes are an excellent source of vitamin C as well as of a number of the B vitamins. They are divided into three groups – earlies, second earlies (or mid-season potatoes) and maincrop ones – depending on how long they take to mature. Although potatoes are generally thought of as a large-scale staple crop, earlies are well worth growing in containers, as they are expensive in the shops at this time. Pressure on space tends to preclude growing maincrop potatoes. Early potatoes are easy to grow but do need a fairly sunny spot to do well. Traditionally, potatoes are planted on Good Friday, but you can, in fact, carry on planting them well into summer, and indeed doing so will give you 'new' potatoes into the autumn.

VARIETIES   There are many unusual varieties of potato, as well as the commonly grown ones. Choose double-certified seed potatoes, guaranteed to be both organic and free from viruses and diseases. Earlies take around 80 to 100 days to mature. Good varieties for containers are: 'Belle de Fontenay': this classic French salad potato, first introduced in 1855, has yellow flesh and a waxy texture; 'Charlotte': another French potato, also good for salads, with waxy flesh; 'Kestrel': a second early introduced in 1992, with good disease resistance; 'Pink Fir Apple': an oddly shaped, pink-skinned potato with good flavour but it can be difficult to grow; 'Remarka': a Dutch variety introduced in 1992 with creamy flesh and slightly waxy; good disease resistance; 'Wilja': another popular Dutch potato, which offers a high yield and is very reliable.

A container of potatoes has been tipped out, showing how the potatoes develop up the stems of the plant. For this reason, earthing up is essential as the plants continue to grow.

CONTAINER SIZE

You can grow potatoes in any deep container. Old buckets, chimney pots and wine barrels are ideal. Allow a depth of at least 45cm (18in) so that you can earth up (see below) the potatoes as the shoots grow. Plant about five potatoes in a 45cm (18in) diameter pot.

CULTIVATION

Buy seed potatoes in early spring and keep them in a cool, dry place to sprout (chit, in technical terminology). This will take a month or so. Once the sprouts are about 2.5cm (1in) long, you can plant the tubers in containers, with the shoot pointing upwards, on a bed of compost about 15cm (6in) deep. Cover them with another 15cm (6in) of compost, and carry on covering them as the shoots grow (this process is known as earthing up). The potatoes form from the sides of the growing stem in a pyramid formation.

If light reaches them, the tubers will turn green (thanks to the presence of a chemical called solanin, which is poisonous), hence the need to keep earthing up the stems. Keep the container well watered throughout this period, to ensure that the potatoes swell to their full size. Provide an organic feed every couple of weeks.

Soil-planted potatoes are subject to a number of soil-borne diseases, from which container-grown potatoes are free, fortunately. The only possible disease in a container is potato blight, which caused the famine in Ireland in the 19th century, but in practice it does not seem to occur if you grow earlies.

HARVESTING

Once they flower (roughly three months after planting), the potatoes should be fully formed; you can dig up one plant to check progress (or scrabble around to find the first potato without digging up the whole plant). Remember that you can store any potatoes that you do not want to use immediately in a cool, dark place.

POTATOES FOR THE TABLE

Don't peel potatoes. Scrub them and cook them in their skins, where most of the vitamins are concentrated. Different varieties of potato are best for particular dishes: waxy potates such as 'Charlotte' are excellent for salads and for sautéeing.

sautéed potatoes with garlic and rosemary

This simple dish is delicious and the aroma as it cooks is almost the best part. Simply scrub some new potatoes and boil them in salted water until just tender. Then heat a couple of tablespoonsful of good-quality olive oil in a frying pan, add 3 chopped cloves of garlic, a couple of sprigs of rosemary and the seasoning. Add the potatoes, roughly chopped or sliced, and cook over a medium heat until the potatoes start to crisp and turn colour. Serve immediately.

450g (1lb) waxy potatoes
2–3 tbs extra virgin olive oil
3 cloves of garlic
2 sprigs of rosemary
seasoning

warm potato salad

This recipe has been a long-standing favourite with family and friends. It provides a light meal, supper or lunch, or a good starter.

Boil the potatoes, with a little salt, until just tender (about 20 minutes). Twelve minutes after putting the potatoes on to boil, put the four eggs on to boil in cold water, and five minutes after that, put the beans onto boil in lightly salted boiling water. In a large bowl, place torn pieces of lettuce as a base. Peel the eggs and cut into quarters, chop the potatoes into rings or quarters, and put the beans in whole. Halve the tomatoes and then add the anchovies, garlic, olives and seasoning. Dress with a lemon vinaigrette (6 tbs good olive oil, 2tbs lemon juice, 1/4 tsp Dijon mustard, pinch of sugar and salt).

450g (1lb) waxy salad potatoes
4 eggs
225g (8oz) French beans
1 crisp lettuce
225g (8oz) cherry tomatoes
1 tin of anchovies
2 cloves of garlic, crushed
handful of black olives
seasoning
lemon vinaigrette dressing

onion family

onions (*allium cepa*), leeks (*a. porrum*), garlic (*a. sativum*)

Although growing large onions is less useful if you are gardening in a confined space, you can successfully grow smaller versions of this valuable family of plants. They include spring onions (immature onions), pickling onions and shallots (*A. cepa*), as well as leeks (*A. porrum*), which you can harvest small, and garlic (*A. sativum*). All members of this family produce swollen leaf bases or bulbs. They are a useful source of vitamin C and phytochemicals, as well as containing vitamin A, calcium and iron. Members of the onion family need a sunny spot to ripen well.

VARIETIES
onions   'Red Baron': red-skinned with mild flavour; 'Golden Bear': early-maturing with good disease resistance.
spring onions and shallots   'White Lisbon': popular and can be grown successfully; 'Long Red Florence': long with red skins.
leeks   'Musselburgh': very hardy.
garlic   'Christo': produces a good yield; 'Russian Red': hardy, with a good flavour.

CONTAINER SIZE
Salad onions, spring onions and chives (a member of the onion family but a herb, see page 126) will all grow well in small pots or troughs, so they are ideal for a window box. Grow onions, leeks and garlic in a larger container, about 60cm (24in) in diameter and 45cm (18in) deep. Leeks will also do well in a tall, narrow container, such as an old chimney pot. which enables you to earth up the stems as they grow, keeping them long and well blanched.

The onion family does best in slightly alkaline soil, and with less nitrogen than most other vegetables. Add a tablespoon of potash to a standard-sized container (30cm/12in diameter) of organic compost. To grow onions (*A. cepa*), either sow seed or plant sets (small bulbs). If you are planting onion sets, plant them in autumn with the tips just showing above the growing medium. The benefit of growing smaller onions, such as shallots and spring onions, is that you can pack them in closely, making good use of container space and harvest them while they are still immature, before they grow too large. To grow onions from seed,

CULTIVATION

ABOVE LEFT Spring onions will grow well in small pots, no more than 20cm (8in) in diameter.

ABOVE RIGHT Onions can be raised in individual growing blocks.

sow the seed in early spring in well-firmed growing medium for a summer/autumn crop, or in late summer for autumn/winter use. Onions do not like loose soil.

To grow leeks (*A. porrum*), sow the seed in spring and transplant once the seedlings are about 15cm (6in) tall, making a narrow hole with a dibber into which the seedling can be dropped. Keep earthing the plants up to increase the length of the white shank. Space at 10cm (4in) apart for smaller leeks.

To grow garlic, plant the cloves in late autumn, with the tips just below the surface of the growing medium, spacing the cloves approximately 10cm (4in) apart.

Water all plants of the onion family regularly and, once the bulbs start to swell or the stems are lengthening, feed once a month.

Onion fly can be a nuisance but covering the plants with fleece will prevent it from occurring. Mildews and rots can be a problem, too. Allow plenty of room around the containers to increase air circulation.

HARVESTING Harvest garlic, spring onions and shallots in early summer. Harvest onions in autumn and leeks from autumn onwards. You can keep onions and garlic by hanging them up in a cool, dry, well-ventilated place.

STORING ONIONS
String onions or garlic together using a length of raffia or string knotted to make a loop. Then weave the onions (or garlic) stems in and out through the loop, adding a new bulb just above the previous one.

spring onion and bacon flan

This makes a good light supper dish. Serve it with green salad and home-baked bread.

Grease a small flan tin, and line with the pastry. Prick with a fork, weight the base and bake in a hot oven (200°C/400°F/gas mark 6) for 15 minutes. Allow to cool. Grill the bacon until crisp and break into small pieces. Lightly fry the spring onions in a little butter. Beat the eggs. Mix the eggs, cream, bacon and onions together, add the grated cheese and seasoning, and pour into the cooled flan case. Lower the oven temperature a little and cook for 25 minutes until the filling has just set (it should be firm to the touch) and is starting to colour.

225g (8oz) shortcrust pastry (ready made)

4 rashers of bacon

12g (¹/₂oz) butter

bunch of spring onions (8 or so), chopped

2 eggs

150ml (¹/₄pt) sour cream

100g (4oz) cheddar, grated

seasoning to taste

vegetable pancakes

Make the pancake batter by putting the flour and seasoning in a bowl and dropping an egg into a well in the middle. Draw the flour in and then add the milk gradually to make a smooth paste. Thin out with milk to the consistency of double cream. Allow the batter to stand for half an hour, and then cook the pancakes in a pre-heated oiled frying pan. Cook the pancakes for a minute or two each side. Turn each pancake onto a plate, and place a sheet of greaseproof paper between each one.

for the vegetable filling
Fry the onion and garlic until golden and soft, and add whatever cold cooked vegetables you have: mangetout peas, beans, spinach, kale, finely sliced carrot and so on. Allow to heat for 3–4 minutes, then add half the single cream, half the Parmesan and the herbs, and stir. Cook for another few minutes, and then pour the mixture on top of each pancake, roll and cover with the remaining Parmesan and a knob of butter. Place in a greased ovenproof dish, pour over the remaining cream and bake in a preheated oven (200°C/400°F/gas mark 6) for 15 minutes.

FOR THE PANCAKES

100g (4oz) plain flour

1 large egg

300ml (¹/₂pt) milk

25g (1oz) butter

seasoning to taste

FOR THE FILLING

1 red onion

2 cloves of garlic

350g (12oz) or so of cooked vegetables, finely sliced

300ml (¹/₂pt) single cream

4 tbs Parmesan cheese

1 tbs mixed fresh herbs

seasoning

knob of butter

carrots
daucus carota

A deep window box in a sunny position makes the ideal place to grow carrots. Here 'Amsterdam' carrots have just been pulled.

Hardy biennials, grown as annuals, carrots are full of vitamin A and are a valuable source of other vitamins (B, C, D, E and K) and potassium. They do well in containers where it is possible to provide the loose, rich soil that they like. There is a wide range of varieties to choose from, some orange, some yellow, some traditionally long, some round. If you harvest them small, they will be ready in 10–12 weeks.

VARIETIES

There are early-maturing, maincrop and late-maturing carrots. The first two are most useful for container growing. 'Paris Market' group: small round carrots, which are quick to mature; 'Amsterdam': slender carrots with smooth skins, also early maturing; 'Chantenay Red-cored': slightly stumpy carrots for early crops; 'James Scarlet Intermediate': medium-sized maincrop; 'Autumn Long': large, late-maturing carrots.

CONTAINER SIZE

Large, long carrots need a deep container, such as an old chimney pot, for example, to allow room for the roots to develop to their full size, although smaller early carrots can be grown in shallower containers, but ideally they should be at least 23cm (9in) deep.

CULTIVATION

You can extend the season for fresh carrots by sowing in early spring and placing a cloche over the container or by sowing in late summer and using a cloche in early autumn. Be aware that carrots are slow

germinators in lower temperatures and need a temperature of at least 7°C (45°F) to get going. Seeds can be sown without protection from mid-spring to early summer. Sow the seed 1cm (½in) deep and thin to 8cm (3in) apart (the thinnings are good in salads). Not all the carrots will grow to the same size, and you will find you have some fully grown ones and some less well-formed ones. The foliage is pretty, so you can sow the seed with annual flowers and grow the carrots in a mixed ornamental and vegetable container if you wish. Water carrots regularly to prevent the roots from splitting, but overwatering can cause too much leaf growth at the expense of root formation.

Carrot fly is a serious problem with major crops of carrots because the flies are attracted by the smell of the foliage. However, new resistant varieties are not being developed. Container-grown carrots do not seem to suffer as badly as crops grown in open ground, but growing the carrots under fleece will prevent the problem.

HARVESTING

Harvest the carrots as they reach an appropriate size. Water the container before harvesting those carrots that have grown to maturity so that you do not disturb the remaining ones.

CARROTS FOR THE TABLE

Carrot salads, of one sort or another, make use of the sweetness and crunchiness of young carrots. A good combination consists of carrot, watercress and mustard and cress. You will need twice the quantity of carrots and watercress to the mustard and cress. Wash and dry the watercress, remove any coarse stalks and break the rest into smaller pieces. Grate the carrot, snip off the mustard and cress and mix all the ingredients together. Dress the salad with a good lemon vinaigrette (see page 35). If you make a larger quantity of vinaigrette than you need, keep what is left in a screwtop jar in the fridge. It will keep for a few days.

beetroot

beta vulgaris

Beetroots are a rich source of vitamin C and folic acid, and are also a source of potassium. They do best in cooler weather because the plants are inclined to bolt (set flowers) in hotter conditions. Some varieties have been developed with bolt resistance, however, and these can be grown later in the year. Sow them in succession for a ready supply for summer salads. The beetroot will be ready roughly 10 weeks after sowing if you harvest them small (5cm/2in) in diameter.

VARIETIES

Beetroots can be round or long and red-, white- or yellow-fleshed.
round 'Boltardy': a bolt-resistant early beetroot with deep red flesh; 'Burpee's Golden': orange skin with yellow flesh (you can use the leaves as greens); 'Albina Veredura' (also sold as 'Snowhite'): white flesh.
long 'Cylindra': an oval-shaped beetroot with deep red flesh; 'Cheltenham Green Top': a long tapering shape; grow it in a deep container.

CULTIVATION

Beet seeds are, in fact, composed of a cluster of seeds. However, you can buy pelleted seed that will create single plants and is therefore more economical, as it requires less thinning. Make several sowings of beetroot for continuous supplies, sowing 8cm (3in) apart. The seeds are quite large and therefore easy to handle, but you can plant them more closely and then thin out unwanted seedlings. If you sow some seed in

early spring and cover it with a cloche (a large clear-plastic bottle cut down makes a good home-made version) you can harvest them small in early summer. Make the other sowings in late spring or early summer for early- and late-summer harvesting. Apply organic fertilizer once a month and keep the compost moist at all times.

Birds may take the young seedlings, so protect them with netting or a bird scarer.

HARVESTING

Pull the beetroot at different stages of development for a variety of sizes. To harvest them, fork them up carefully and twist off the tops. Do not cut them or they will bleed. You can use the young leaves in salads.

BEETROOT FOR THE TABLE

Beetroot are normally cooked in their skins, so simply scrub them first and then boil them in lightly salted water until they are tender – usually about 20 minutes for small beetroot, 30 minutes for larger ones. Beetroot goes very well with sour cream and chives. Make a simple salad with these ingredients or make a hot dish by slicing the beetroot in rings and layering them in a small buttered ovenproof dish. Pour enough crème fraîche over the beetroot to cover and bake in a moderate oven for 15 minutes. Sprinkle the surface with chopped chives and parsley or coriander. Serve warm but not piping hot.

If you grow different coloured beetroot, you can make a colourful salad using sliced beetroot on a bed of young beetroot, rocket and radish leaves, for example, or any other mix of young green leaves. Dress with a light lemony vinaigrette (see page 35).

There are a number of good varieties of beetroot that will grow well in containers. These are 'Pronto', which can be harvested from midsummer onwards.

chard

beta vulgaris cicla group

This is a member of the spinach family, all of which will grow in containers if you wish. It provides a valuable source of vitamin C and iron. Ruby chard, with its blood-red leafstalks and mid-ribs, is the most attractive, so is a good choice in limited space. Swiss chard has thick white mid-ribs and leafstalks. All the spinach family have similarly fleshy green leaves, and they all make deep roots, so give them an unusually deep container for best results. Unlike many vegetables, chard and spinach will do well in light shade, so can be useful in limited space. Winter spinach (*Spinacea oleracea*) is particularly useful, as it will provide you with a crop when there is not much else around.

VARIETIES There are a few different sorts of ruby and Swiss chard, but spinaches are rarely listed. 'Ruby Chard': the best known, with brilliant red mid-ribs and leaf veins, is ornamental as well as edible; 'Rainbow Bright Lights': orange, red and yellow mid-ribs and leaf veins; 'Fordhook Giant': prolific, larger than usual, robust Swiss chard.

CONTAINER SIZE A container at least 30cm (12in) in diameter and 30cm (12in) deep is the best size for these strongly growing vegetables. You can plant two to three in a pot 30cm (12in) across.

CULTIVATION Sow seed of chard and summer spinach 1cm (1/2in) deep in mid-spring, two or three to a 30cm (12in) pot, and, when the seedlings are large enough to handle, thin them out to around 23cm (9in) apart. Avoid overcrowding as it encourages mildew (as I found to my cost when I tried to maximize the space in my containers!). Sow spinach seed in the same way: summer spinach can be sown from mid-spring to late spring; winter spinach is sown from late summer for a winter crop. Spinach requires plenty of nitrogen, so topdress with an organic fertilizer during growth. You can grow spinach as a cut-and-come-again seedling crop (leaving about 8cm/3in between plants all round), using the young leaves in salads. Keep well watered at all times. Feed with liquid fertilizer once a month.

Do not grow close to other plants from the courgette/cucumber family as they are all susceptible to the same viruses.

Pull individual leaves when required. Use the smallest leaves for salads with other salad greens (see page 62–9).

BELOW There are various varieties of chard, but generally those with the most colourful mid-ribs are the best value for containers, as they are good to look at, too. The colour in young rainbow chard (below left) has still to develop; in a mature plant (below right) the mid-ribs are a rich orange-red.

HARVESTING

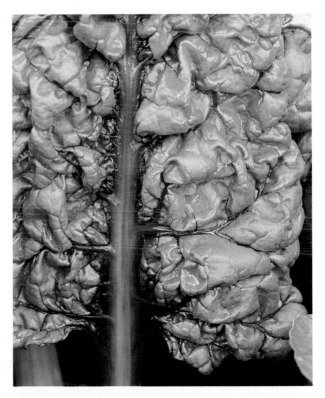

cabbage, kale
brassica oleracea capitata group

These are among the most nutritious vegetables you can grow, but are somewhat despised by many. However, even if you do not particularly want to eat them, they make interesting-looking plants, and I find them beautiful (a legacy from drawing them as an art student). You can grow them in early spring for autumn harvests and in summer for winter harvests. Those described as spring cabbage have looser leaves and are sown in summer for an early-spring harvest. As your available space is probably taken up in spring and summer with more worthwhile crops, winter cabbages could be a good choice (when everything else has been harvested). Kales are the hardiest members of the brassica family, and their flavour improves after frost.

VARIETIES

autumn cabbages 'Cuor di Bue'; 'Red Drumhead'.
winter cabbages 'January King'; 'Vertus'.
dwarf kale 'Green Curled'; 'Redbor'; 'Russian Red'.

CONTAINER SIZE

Plant one cabbage or kale plant in each 20cm (8in) diameter container, or three in a large window box or grow bag.

CULTIVATON

Sow seed in late spring to early summer, three to a pot, and thin out to the best seedling in each. Use bird-scaring devices to protect young cabbage seedlings, or cloches to prevent slug and snail damage. Many flying insects are attracted to them, so cover them with fleece in the early stages if you can. Cabbages, rather more than kales, need plenty of nitrogen, so feed regularly with nitrogen-rich fertilizer and keep moist at all times. Cabbages attract pests so be on your guard! Take preventive measures (cloches help young seedlings) and sow more than one crop successively to ensure you have a reserve crop if all else fails. Planting marigolds deters whitefly while the marigolds are still strongly growing.

Cut cabbages when the head has fully hearted up. Kale leaves can be cut as required with secateurs or sharp scissors.

Cabbage is delicious sliced thinly as a salad with a mayonnaise dressing and it is equally good braised with onions, garlic, sultanas and juniper berries. For the latter, sweat the vegetables in a little butter, add the other ingredients and some seasoning, together with a few tablespoons of water, and simmer gently until tender. Add chopped parsley just before serving. It makes the ideal accompaniment to boiled ham.

BELOW, FROM LEFT TO RIGHT
Cabbage 'January King', 'Dwarf Green Curled' kale and young cabbages planted with French marigolds, in the hope of deterring whitefly.

HARVESTING

CABBAGE FOR THE TABLE

radishes

raphanus sativus

Radishes can be be grown as a summer or winter crop. The summer-harvested radishes are small and mature fast. The winter radishes are larger. Both kinds can be either round (about 4cm/1¹/2in in diameter) or cylindrical (about 5cm/2in or even longer). The skin can be red or white, or even yellow or black in some varieties, but the flesh is white, peppery and crisp. The 'hot' flavour becomes more marked if the radishes are not watered frequently. Radishes are a useful source of both vitamin C and potassium.

VARIETIES

There are many to choose from: **summer radishes** 'Cherry Belle Round': red skin; 'French Breakfast': long with red skin and white tips; 'Scarlet Globe': round with red skin; 'White Icicle': long with white skin. **winter radishes** 'China Rose': long, with red skin; 'Noir de Paris': long with brown skin.

CONTAINER SIZE

Pretty much any container will take a few radishes, even a small 23cm (9in) diameter pot or a window box. Equally, because they grow quickly, they can share a larger container with later-maturing vegetables, such as beans.

CULTIVATION

Sow summer radishes from spring onwards, in succession, to ensure a regular supply for salads. Sow winter radishes in midsummer. Spring-sown radishes can be grown in full sun, but summer-sown radishes for winter use are best grown in partial shade. You need to sow radishes at an even depth of about 1cm (¹/₂in). Thin summer radishes to 8cm (3in) apart, winter radishes to 10cm (4in) apart, and use the thinnings in salads. (Radishes do not transplant well.) As radishes grow quickly, they can become leggy if too closely spaced and the roots then fail to develop properly, or some will and others won't. If the compost has too much nitrogen, you will get too much leaf at the expense of the root. Because they mature fast, they are usually pest and disease free, although cabbage root fly and flea beetle can be problems.

The crop will be ready within four to eight weeks of sowing, depending on the variety.

HARVESTING

Radishes are delicious served as a simple starter on their own, particularly when they are very fresh and neither too hot nor too dry. Wash the radishes well, twist off the leaves, and chill them in the fridge for an hour. Serve whole with really cold unsalted butter and very fresh French bread. Alternatively, serve sliced with other salad ingredients, such as carrot, apple and watercress.

RADISHES FOR THE TABLE

FAR LEFT 'French Breakfast' radishes have long, red- and white-skinned cylindrical roots, which make good use of container space.

LEFT 'Cherry Belle' round, red-skinned radishes have good flavour.

peas

pisum sativum

'Meteor': a first early pea which crops well, and is therefore a good choice for container growing.

This relatively fast-growing annual is a valuable source of vitamins C and B1, as well as valuable phytochemicals and folic acid. When growing them in the open, you have the choice of first or second earlies, or maincrop peas, but for container growing, where space is limited, you may prefer mangetout or sugar snap peas, of which both the pod and the peas are eaten and which have greater flavour. Peas are natural climbers, using small leaf petioles to do so; you will need to create a support system for them, such as bamboo canes with wires and/or strings stretched horizontally between the canes.

VARIETIES

'Meteor': a first early pea; 'Sugar Snap': a high-yielding, taller-growing pea with good flavour: 'Sugar Rae': a snap pea; not as productive as 'Sugar Snap' but grows less tall; 'Norli': a mangetout pea, with a dwarf habit and a good yield; 'Early Onward': a first early pea; 'Pilot': a maincrop pea with a good cropping period; 'Purple Podded': a maincrop pea with decorative purple pods.

CONTAINER SIZE

You can grow approximately eight pea plants in a 30cm (12in) container. To get a good crop, plant up either two containers of this size or one larger container roughly 45cm (18in) in diameter.

CULTIVATION

Sow first peas indoors in mid-spring, 1.5cm (3/4in) deep in small pots. You can continue to sow outdoor at intervals in late spring and early summer, provided you sow a mildew-resistant variety in summer. It is worth sowing more than once, since peas can succumb to a variety of

problems (see below). Once the peas have reached roughly 8cm (3in) in height, they can be planted out, provided all danger of frosts has passed, or cover with a cloche if the weather turns cold. Harden off the young plants (see page 20) and then transplant them into their full-size container, and provide the basis of the support system, such as a cone of canes tied into a wigwam shape. You can invent all manner of supports, from chicken wire to netting, but the peas will also need lateral supports, as well as vertical ones, at fairly frequently spaced intervals, to which the small tendrils can cling. Keep them well watered and feed them once a month.

Unfortunately, peas can attract both pests and diseases. Birds are singularly keen on the seeds, as are mice, which should be less of a problem when peas are grown in containers, particularly on a balcony. String brightly coloured foil (bottle tops or similar) above plants as a bird scarer. Damping off diseases can attack early sowings, and pea moth (the cause of the grubs I so loathed to find when shelling peas as a child) may attack later ones.

HARVESTING

Remove the entire pod for sugar snap and mangetout peas, snipping it off at the stem. They should be ready 11 weeks after sowing. Shelling peas will be ready 12–16 weeks after sowing. They should be harvested as soon as the pods bulge noticeably. If you leave them too long, the peas may become hard and dry.

PEAS FOR THE TABLE

Mangetout peas are delicious. To enjoy them at their best, serve them very lightly cooked, as a stir fry. Heat a little oil in a wok, add the mangetout with a small amount of grated fresh ginger and shredded garlic and stir briskly for a few minutes until tender but still crisp.

beans

Of all the vegetables you can grow, beans are among the most deserving of your precious space. They are full of protein (an excellent source of it if you are vegetarian) and generally they are undemanding plants to grow. From a container gardener's point of view, the beans worth growing are those eaten fresh, either the whole pod or the beans within: runner, French and broad beans are the best for this purpose. Other beans in the family are soya and lima beans, the beans of which are normally dried, and, oddly, peanuts. Mung beans can be eaten as sprouts, and are extremely nutritious, so they are certainly worth growing. All you need to do is soak the beans overnight in warm water, rinse them and then spread them on damp cottonwool. Cover with clingfilm and brown paper. Between six to nine days later the sprouts will be a couple of inches long and ready to use.

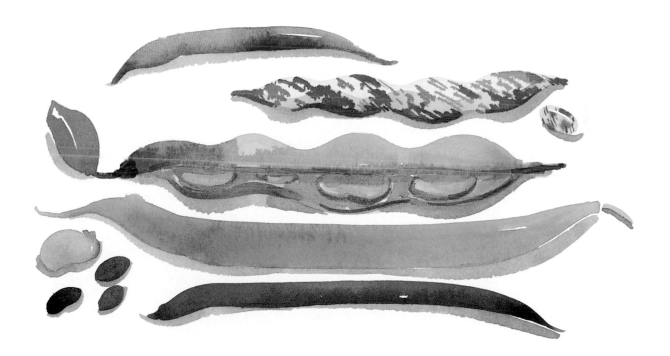

runner beans

phaseolus coccineus

Perennials grown as annuals in cooler climates, runner beans are useful if your garden is slightly shady, as they will grow well in less sunny conditions than other beans. They grow on vines that will reach up to 4.2m (14ft), if allowed to do so and need a strong support system (you can pinch out the tops when several trusses of flowers have formed to keep them to more manageable proportions). One of the great advantages of growing runner beans is that they produce a mass of attractive flowers (which are also edible).

VARIETIES

There are a number of good varieties, including 'Desiree': stringless beans with good flavour and white flowers; 'Hammond Dwarf Scarlet': a bush variety that needs no support; 'Painted Lady': not the best beans but singularly pretty red and white flowers; 'Scarlet Emperor': a very popular bean with scarlet flowers, and a heavy cropper with a very good flavour.

CULTIVATION

Sow the seeds (the beans themselves) indoors roughly two or three weeks before the usual last frosts in your area. Sow each seed about 5cm (2in) deep. Transplant them into their permanent container once all danger of frost has passed. Plant roughly four or five beans to a container approximately 30cm (12in) in diameter. Insert a long (at least 1.5m/5ft) cane at each station and tie the tops together to form a wigwam effect. (Alternatively, plant the beans in a long trough and support them using strings tied to a wall.) The beans will twine themselves around the supports. If they outgrow the structure and you already have several flower trusses on each plant, pinch out the growing tip (see tomatoes, page 72) to keep them under control.

Keep the compost moist at all times, because if you forget to water the beans will become tough and stringy. Feed once a fortnight with a general organic fertilizer once the beans start to form.

Slugs and snails may attack the young plants, so go out at night with a torch and remove them before they do any damage. Aphids will also attack young shoots, so spray the plants with insecticidal soap at the first signs of an attack.

HARVESTING

Pick the beans regularly when they are small (about 10 weeks after sowing). Hold the main stem in one hand while you pull each bean off with the other, otherwise you may inadvertently tug the whole plant out. Runner beans taste better and are much more tender when they are young; regular picking will encourage more bean pods to form. If you grow more than you can eat, you can freeze them, but they are not the best vegetable for the freezer, becoming slightly flabby in the freezing process. Whole French beans freeze much better.

french beans
phaseolus vulgaris

Although you can eat the seeds of French beans, they are really only worthwhile growing in containers for their fresh, young pods, which are eaten whole. They come in bush (dwarf) and climbing forms. Both are suitable for containers. They need more sunshine than runner beans and the climbing forms will need similar supports, such as a wigwam of bamboo canes.

VARIETIES

Different varieties have variously shaped (round or flat) and coloured pods (green, gold, or purple). 'Blue Lake': a round, green climbing bean

which produces a good crop and the beans can also be dried as haricots; 'The Prince': a dwarf, flat bean; 'Kinghorn Wax': a yellow-podded climbing bean with good flavour; 'Royal Burgundy': a purple-podded dwarf bean.

Climbing French beans, such as 'Cobra', need a similar support structure to runner beans, although they do not grow as tall.

You can get a crop of beans from even smallish containers (25cm/10in in diameter) which will allow between six and eight beans per pot.

CONTAINER SIZE

As for runner beans (see page 56).

CULTIVATION

Unlike runner beans, French beans will freeze well if you have surplus crop. Remember to blanch them for a minute or so in boiling water before freezing them.

HARVESTING

broad beans
vicia faba

Unlike the other beans, broad beans are hardy and can be overwintered if you wish. They are extremely nutritious and, along with potatoes, have long been a staple peasant crop. However, not everyone likes them. Eating them while they are still very young is the secret. Once they are older, the skin encasing the individual beans becomes tough and bitter. I can remember diligently removing these as a child before being prepared to eat the much sweeter kernel of each bean!

You can plant the seeds in either autumn or spring. Autumn sowing means they get away to an early start and often avoid attacks of blackfly, for which the young shoots are a great attraction.

There are dwarf bush beans (to 30cm/12in tall) as well as the standard-sized ones which grow to about 1.2m (4ft) tall. In addition, there are both

VARIETIES

long-podded beans and short-podded ones. The shorter podded ones are deemed to have the best flavour. 'Green Windsor': a short-podded variety with green beans; 'White Windsor': similar but with white beans; 'The Sutton': a dwarf bush bean; 'Bonny Lad': another dwarf bean, but slightly taller (around 38cm/15in) than 'The Sutton'.

CONTAINER SIZE   Grow in a 25cm (10in) diameter container.

CULTIVATION   Sow the beans in either late autumn or early spring (a couple of months after Christmas), about 5cm (2in) deep and about 10cm (4in) apart in a container with a good depth of compost (at least 20cm/8in). On a windy site it may be worth giving the young plants some support as they grow – put in a few canes around the perimeter of the pot and tie them with string about 15cm (6in) up. Keep well watered.

Broad beans are sometimes vulnerable to chocolate spot, for which there is no remedy. Pull up the plants and burn them. Don't go for autumn sowing if this happens to your crop because autumn-sown plants are more vulnerable. Aphids are the other possible problem; spray with insecticidal soap or simply rub them off with your fingers. If the beans are well grown when the attack occurs, pinch out the tips, which are the major attraction.

HARVESTING   Pick when the pods are still relatively small (no more than 15cm/6in long). Autumn- or early-spring-sown varieties will be ready from early summer onwards. If you pick them when they are small (around 8cm/3in) you can eat both the pod and the bean, as you would mangetout peas. To harvest beans, hold the stem with one hand and pick the beans with the other to avoid pulling up the whole plant.

beans in garlic

Cook the beans in lightly salted water until just tender. Then melt a small knob of butter in the pan, stir in the garlic and seasoning, and toss the beans in it for a minute or so before serving.

350g (12oz) French beans or shelled broad beans

knob of butter

2 cloves of garlic, crushed

seasoning

tagliatelle with baby courgettes, baby broad beans and mangetout peas

Heat the olive oil in a heavy-based frying pan, and fry the garlic until golden. Add the tagliatelle to a pan of boiling salted water and cook for 3–4 minutes. Meanwhile, add the vegetables to the garlic and cook for a few more minutes until barely soft. Add the cream and lemon juice and allow to warm.

Drain the tagliatelle, tip the vegetables into the centre and sprinkle with grated Parmesan and longer curls of Parmesan and torn basil. Serve with rocket salad.

3 tbs olive oil

3 cloves of garlic, crushed

450g (1lb) fresh tagliatelle

handful each of baby courgettes, sliced, shelled broad beans and mangetout peas

150ml (1/4pt) single cream

2 tbs lemon juice

4 tbs Parmesan

basil

S A L A D
L E A V E S

All manner of leaves make interesting salad ingredients, so it is worth growing as wide a range as possible. They are often called salad greens, but this name is something of a misnomer, since there is now an increasingly wide range of interesting colours to add to the panoply of edible leaves. Apart from their nutritional content, salads of more varied leaves add zest to any meal and are a useful source of vitamin C, as well as A and B. For those of us raised on the 'wilting lettuce, slice of beetroot and hard-boiled egg' concept of a salad, it is something of a leap of faith to start eating radish leaves and vegetable thinnings, but once converted you will not look back!

With limited space in which to grow salad leaves, it pays to think successionally, so that as one crop finishes, another is just about ready for the table. With a little careful planning, and the use of a cloche or two, you should be able to enjoy fresh leaves all year round.

The staple of any salad is nearly always lettuce, in one form or another, so this makes a good place to start.

Young 'Little Gem' cos lettuces grown in a box. As they mature rapidly – in a matter of a few weeks – you can grow them in any container, such as this former fruit basket.

lettuce

lactuca sativa

Lettuces are extremely varied in taste, texture, appearance and flavour. From a grower's point of view, they are grouped into several major categories. In one group are the cabbage-type lettuces that form a round heart and can be either soft-leaved (butterhead) or crisp (crisphead). In another is the cos lettuce, which has an elongated appearance with crispish leaves and heart. There is an intermediate group, which is a cross between the former two types, and there is yet another group, the loose-leafed lettuces, that do not form a heart but have frilly leaves that are plucked as required.

BELOW (LEFT TO RIGHT)
'Continuity', a butterhead lettuce, 'Paris Island', a cos type, and 'Valdarz', a loose-leafed lettuce.

You can grow lettuces in containers as small as 15cm (6in) in diameter, one to a pot. Alternatively, plant a row of them in a window box. You can also interplant them among other taller vegetables, making good use of available container space.

There is a wide range of lettuce varieties to choose from, and it is well worth growing several different types, as well as ensuring that you have a continual supply over a long season.

early-spring sowings 'Little Gem': cos; 'Tom Thumb': butterhead; 'Ithaca': crisphead.

later sowings (slow-to-bolt varieties) 'Buttercrunch': cos/butterhead cross; 'Webb's Wonderful': crisphead; 'Salad Bowl': loose leaf.

autumn sowings 'Winter Density': cos; 'Brune d'Hiver': butterhead; 'Marvel of Four Seasons': loose leaf.

Although lettuces naturally mature in the summer, new varieties have been bred that will overwinter ready for an early crop the following summer. Sow the seed of all lettuces thickly and cover with a fine layer of potting compost. Thin them once they are 5cm (2in) tall. Make the first sowings in early spring indoors and plant out under cloches. Make successional sowings outdoors throughout the spring and summer. Winter-hardy lettuces can be sown in autumn and will be ready early next summer. Water lettuces copiously and frequently. Feed once a month. Lettuces are generally disease free but they are susceptible to slug and snail damage.

If you are planting 'cut-and-come-again' lettuce, sow the seeds about 2.5cm (1in) apart in all directions, do not thin, and cut off the leaves at the base when they are 10cm (4in) high. Cos lettuce do well grown in this way, particularly 'Paris White Cos' or 'Paris Island Cos', according to Joy Larkcom (*Vegetables for Small Gardens*).

Either cut individual leaves once they are a few inches tall, as you require them, or harvest whole heads approximately 10 weeks after sowing.

other salad leaves

There are two kinds of Chinese cabbage, one that forms a head and another that doesn't, known as pak choi. The latter type is the best to grow. It has pale, crunchy leaves that are good for stir fries. Different cultivars vary in height from just 10cm (4in) to almost 60cm (2ft), but the dwarf-growing ones make good container plants. Sow the seed under cover in mid-spring or outdoors in late spring. Later sowings will be inclined to bolt. You can cut the seedlings four to five weeks after sowing as a cut-and-come-again crop. They require copious watering. Harvest whole heads 10 weeks after sowing. They are subject to the same range of pests and diseases as ordinary cabbages (see page 48). Two bolt-resistant cultivars are 'Chingensai', which has green stems, and 'Joi Choi', which has white stems.

chinese cabbage
brassica rapa var. *chinensis*

The flat-leaved chicories (*C. intybus*) and the curly-leaved form (*C. endivia*), known as endive, can be used in salads or as a cooked vegetable; the leaves are grown for salads, and the roots are cooked. There are many different forms and colours. The flowers, a pretty blue, are edible and can also be used in salads (see pages 132–5). The leaves are bitter and will normally require blanching once they are full size to make them palatable, but you can pick the young leaves for salads. Grow the red-leaved chichories (often labelled on seed packets as *radicchio*, the Italian name for chicory) to add colour to your salads. Sow the seed just after the last frosts have passed and carry on sowing every couple of weeks until late summer. Cut the leaves when they are about 8cm (3in) tall. Water well and feed occasionally to encourage more leaves to grow.

chicory
cichorium spp.

Pak choi, one of many different types of Chinese greens, is a useful, easy-to-grow leafy vegetable with a crunchy texture. It is good for both stir fries and salads.

rocket
eruca sativa

Rocket by name and rocket by nature, this hot and spicy salad vegetable is a very fast-growing salad crop, which will quickly bolt in hot weather. Sow seed in early spring to prevent this or make successional sowings in partial shade. It does well, too, interplanted with larger vegetables to save space. Sow the seed fairly thickly on the surface of the compost and keep moist to prevent bolting. If you succeed in keeping the container moist at all times, you can use rocket as a cut-and-come-again crop; It will re-sprout a couple of times. If a pot does run to seed, you can save the seed for the following year's supply.

Rocket, one of the fastest-growing and easiest salad crops to grow, adds spice to blander-tasting salad leaves.

These grow extremely easily, even on damp cardboard or blotting paper, and are particularly good for adding flavour to sandwiches or egg dishes. Sow the seed thickly and evenly in wide-diameter, fairly shallow, containers, on pre-moistened compost, but do not cover with soil. Cover the top of the container to encourage germination and move into the light once the seedlings are roughly 2.5cm (1in) high. Cut when 5cm (2in) tall. Mustard germinates more quickly than cress, so if you want both together, sow the mustard a few days later than the cress. Let one pot run to seed and collect the seeds for next year's crop.

mustard and cress
sinapsis alba

Particularly useful on account of its hardiness, corn salad (sometimes known as lamb's lettuce) has mild-flavoured, small, rounded leaves. A small plant, growing to no more than 15cm (6in) all around, it can be planted with taller vegetables. It is relatively slow growing. Sow it in early summer for an autumn or winter crop – it will take roughly three months to mature – or use it sooner as a cut-and-come-again crop. Corn salad will over-winter in relatively cold climates, but a cloche will improve the leaf texture. 'Verte de Cambrai' and 'Verte d'Etapes' are both very hardy cultivars.

corn salad
valerianella locusta

If you opt for the cut-and-come-again method of harvesting salad vegetables, you will be able to pick salad leaves over a long season. Make sure when you wash them that you dry them throroughly, as wet lettuce and dressing do not go well together. Mix the ingredients for whatever dressing you prefer (see page 138) and toss the salad in the dressing just before serving.

SALAD LEAVES FOR THE TABLE

tomatoes

lycopersicon esculentum

The tomato, a tender perennial, is native to South America and was introduced into Europe in the 16th century. In their natural habitat tomato plants grow very vigorously and fruit copiously, but in colder climates you may have to coax them into fruiting well if there are inadequate levels of sunshine after the plants have set fruit. In cold or wet areas, try growing them under a cloche or bringing them indoors to a conservatory or a position in front of a sunny window. Nonetheless, the tomato is one of the best crops to grow in containers, producing abundant supplies from relatively little space, thanks to the plant's climbing habit.

Tomatoes are packed with vitamins and are apparently rich in phytochemicals. Recent research indicates that tomatoes (even when cooked) have great health benefits, including cancer-fighting properties.

VARIETIES

There are three principal types to grow: tall, bush or dwarf. The tall types need training up strings or poles; the bush types will sprawl (and can even be grown in a hanging basket) and the dwarf types form compact miniature bushes, ideal for very tiny spaces but with smaller yields.

There is a wealth of choice from huge beefsteak tomatoes to tiny cherry ones, in a splendid range of colours including yellows, pinks and even white, and some are interestingly striped. Of the varieties of size and type popularly available the following are all worth growing: 'Beefmaster' (beefsteak type); 'Marmande'; 'Gardener's Delight'; and 'Sweet 100'.

CONTAINER SIZE

Containers should be at least 25cm (10in) in diameter and ideally 30cm (12in) deep for each plant. If you prefer, use a grow bag. One large growing bag will take three tomato plants – ample for a two-person household. A family of four might need six plants in two growing bags.

CULTIVATION

Sow three seeds in a small pot in gentle heat in mid-spring. Germination will take about a week. Then thin them down to one seed per pot once they reach the three-leaf stage. Transplant them when they are about 15cm (6in) tall into the growing pot once any danger of frost is past (about six to eight weeks after sowing). Alternatively, you can buy young plants grown in individual pots. Give tall tomatoes a supporting cane (at least 1m/3ft high).

As the tomato plant grows, tie the main stem to the cane loosely, taking care not to damage it. You will need to 'stop' the plant once four or five trusses have appeared (see below) and remove surplus leaves that grow between the sideshoots and the main stem.

1

2

PINCHING OUT

1 Pinch out the non-flower-bearing sideshoots and the basal growths at the point at which the trusses start to form. Tomato plants need warm roots, and too much foliage diverts the energy of the plant, which should be directed into flowering and fruiting.

2 In high summer, when there are four or five trusses of fruit on the plant, pinch out the growing point (the uppermost growth).

Tomatoes need a sunny spot to fruit well. Tall-growing varieties, such as this cherry tomato, should be tied in to a good support system.

Tomatoes in containers need frequent watering, at least a couple of times a week, and more often in hot weather or if grown under glass. Less frequent watering will result in tomatoes with good flavour but very tough skins. Feed the plants with an organic tea (see page 23) once a fortnight until the fruit ripen.

Tomatoes are relatively trouble free, but you might find it worthwhile to plant French marigolds around the base: they look attractive and help to deter whitefly. Put mulch around the base to protect the plants from slugs and to conserve moisture.

HARVESTING

The fruit should be ready to pick in late summer. Any fruit that is still green in early autumn can be taken off the plant, wrapped in paper and stored in a dark drawer (make sure the tomatoes are in good condition at this point or you will end up with a drawer full of mould) or lay them out on a plate. Placing one ripe tomato in a bowl of green ones will help them complete the ripening process more quickly, as ripe tomatoes give off a chemical that encourages the process in neighbouring fruit. Failing that, green tomatoes make excellent chutney (see page 138).

TOMATOES FOR THE TABLE

To get the maximum benefit from tomatoes, and to appreciate their flavour, pick them on a sunny day and eat them raw, straight from the plant. Do not, whatever you do, refrigerate them if you plan to use them in salads, as chilling destroys their flavour. This is particularly true of the smaller tomatoes, such as the cherry types. The bigger beefsteak tomatoes can either be used for salads, or stuffed and baked. Use slightly over-ripe tomatoes for tomato and basil soup (see basic soup recipe, page 139), tomato and pepper pasta sauce (see page 85) or with other vegetables for ratatouille.

tomato and goat's cheese bruschetta

Halve the tomatoes and oven roast them in a warm oven for 30 minutes. Slice the baguette and cook on a rack in the oven for the last 10 minutes. Spread the tomatoes, goat's cheese, garlic and basil leaves on the slices. Drizzle with olive oil and serve warm.

16 cherry tomatoes
1/2 baguette
75g (3oz) goat's cheese, roughly cubed
2 cloves garlic, crushed
small handful of torn basil leaves
3 tbs olive oil

mozzarella and tomato salad

Use good-quality mozzarella for this (buffalo mozzarella for preference). Slice the tomatoes and mozzarella into rings. Lay them on a plate. Either chop the garlic finely or crush it in a garlic crusher if you can be bothered (I find it tedious to clean). Scatter the garlic and basil over the tomatoes. Sprinkle with olive oil and lemon juice; season to taste and garnish with a few olives. Do not refrigerate this salad: it should be served at room temperature, ideally with home-made brown bread.

225g (8oz) tomatoes
225g (8oz) mozzarella cheese
2 large cloves of garlic
1 tbs fresh basil, torn
2 tbs olive oil
1 tbs lemon juice
seasoning
1 tbs black olives

variation
The Portuguese make a similar tomato salad, substituting sliced onions (red onions are ideal, being fairly sweet) in place of the mozzarella, and coriander for the basil.

cucumbers

cucumis sativus

Cucumbers are tender perennials; they come from tropical parts of the world, where they make tremendous growth in a very short space of time. Although the smooth-skinned cucumbers cannot be grown outside in temperate climates, the rougher-skinned, or ridged, cucumbers will do extremely well. Cucumbers provide a good source of vitamins A and C, and potassium. Like other tender vegetables, they are grown in late spring to summer and fruit from midsummer onwards. They need a warm, sunny spot, with shelter from cold winds. A sheet of glass behind the support will help protect the crop and increase the warmth. Gherkins are grown in precisely the same way as cucumbers, but they take up less space and are therefore ideal for containers. Pick them when they are roughly 5cm (2in) long.

VARIETIES

There are a good few cucumbers to choose from, including round as well as the usual long cucumbers.
long cucumber 'Nadir', 'Baton Vert', 'Burpee', 'Patio Pik' (ideal for containers), 'Long Green Ridge'.
round cucumbers 'Marion'.
gherkins 'Bestal'; 'Hokus'; 'Vento Pickling'.

CONTAINER SIZE

You can grow three cucumbers in a standard-sized growing bag or one per pot in a 30cm (12in) deep and wide container. Unless you have a large and hungry family with a passion for cucumbers, one or two plants will be more than adequate for your needs. The best solution is to stagger the planting by a couple of weeks so that your entire crop does not come to fruition at the same time.

If you sow the seeds in mid-spring, under cover, you can put the plants out in early summer after all danger of frost has passed. Sow the large, flat seeds two to a small pot, 8cm (3in) in diameter, and remove the weaker seedling. Harden the young plants off gradually (see page 20) before planting up in a growing bag or larger container. Alternatively, sow the seed outside in early summer, one per pot, with a cloche over the jar to speed growth and protect the emergent seedling from slugs.

CULTIVATION

TRANSPLANTING CUCUMBERS

1 Cucumbers dislike being transplanted, and they dislike firm soil, too. Plant two seeds on edge in each pot.

2 When you transplant them, up-end the small pot and transfer the entire contents to a larger pot with the minimum of root disturbance.

1

2

The cucumber plants will need to be supported on canes or strings in the same way as tomato plants (see page 72) and will make even more vigorous growth. Pinch out the growing point in the same way once there are half a dozen leaves per shoot, to encourage the sideshoots to fruit. Once the fruit start to form, provide a high-potash feed once a fortnight.

Unsurprisingly, as they are made up mostly of water, cucumbers need frequent watering. Keep the soil moist, without waterlogging it. If you fail to water adequately, you will have small, rather tough cucumbers with very bitter skins, if you get any at all.

Cucumber mosaic virus, which presents itself as yellowish mottling on the leaves, can be a problem, about which you can do nothing except destroy the plants. Keep cucumbers away from other members of the *Cucurbitaceae* family, as they are all prone to the disease. If the plants are attacked by red spider mite, which is more likely if they are grown under glass, the foliage becomes rust coloured; if you look very carefully you will see the tiny insects on the undersides of leaves. Frequent misting with water will help to prevent attacks.

HARVESTING

Pick the cucumbers when they are still fairly small – about 15cm (6in) long. They will be ready between eight and ten weeks after planting out. Twist the stalk to remove them from the plant.

CUCUMBERS FOR THE TABLE

Home-grown cucumbers make delicious sandwiches. Potato and cucumber salad is equally good. Scrape the potatoes, boil them until they are just tender and cut them into cubes. Peel and cube the cucumber. Dress with home-made mayonnaise, thinned with cream, and garnish with chopped parsley.

RIGHT AND FAR RIGHT Outdoor cucumbers are not as large as the ones that you can buy in the shops, but they taste better and are surprisingly easy to grow. The flowers (right) make a pretty addition to a salad. Far right, cucumbers ready for harvesting.

courgettes

cucurbita pepo

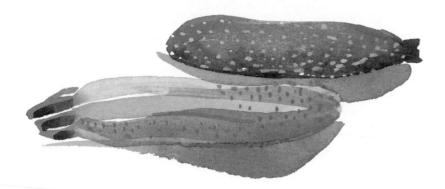

Courgettes are simply immature marrows. They can be found in a marvellous range of colours, shapes and sizes: green, yellow, white, striped, long, round or flat, and they are a significant source of vitamin C, as well as calcium and iron, and vitamin A. There are both bush and trailing forms. The latter are ideal for small spaces because they can be trained vertically up poles or wires, thereby taking up minimal precious ground space. Although you could grow marrows and pumpkins (winter squash), they require more space and are less suitable for container growing than the smaller courgettes.

How much time do you have? Choosing is likely to be the hardest part, so probably the most amount of fun can be obtained by trying different varieties each year, to see which gives you the most pleasure. The odder ones will certainly impress your friends, although there will not be much to choose between them taste-wise. **bush types** (green): 'Early Gem'; 'Zucchini'; 'Diamante'; (gold): 'Golden Courgette'. **trailing** 'Little Gem' (round fruits); 'Long Green Trailing'.

VARIETIES

Plant them in pots 30cm (12in) diameter and 30cm (12in) deep, or plant three plants to a standard growing bag.

CONTAINER SIZE

Sow the seeds, which are large and flat, on edge, two to a 8cm (3in) pot in mid-spring, indoors, in warmth. Plant out after the last frosts in large containers. Cover young plants with a cloche to protect from slugs.

Water generously at all times. Support the trailing types on strings or poles, tying in as necessary to help them climb. Pinch out the leading shoots once the plants reach several feet. When flowers start to form, feed with liquid feed once a fortnight. The plant will produce both male and female flowers, the latter bearing the fruit.

If no fruit sets (cold weather can stop insect activity and natural pollination) you may need to hand pollinate. The female flower has a tiny thickened section of stem just behind the flower. Pick a male flower, remove the petals, and brush the male organ against the centre of the female flowers, as carefully as you can.

As with other members of the *Cucurbitaceac* family, red spider mite and mosaic virus cause problems. Keep spraying plants with water to control red spider mite and burn any affected by mosaic virus.

Pick the courgettes as soon as they are about 10cm (4in) long and keep picking regularly unless you want marrows. The first fruits will form roughly 10–12 weeks after planting.

You can eat very small courgettes raw, sliced in salads. Slightly larger ones are best lightly cooked. One of the best ways to cook them is to slice them lengthways, fairly thinly, and cook them very briefly in boiling, salted water. Drain them and then fry them in olive oil, with crushed garlic and parsley, for a few minutes to brown them. Larger ones still can be baked in the oven with sliced tomatoes. Slice the courgettes and tomatoes in rings and layer them in a greased ovenproof dish, dot with butter, cover with breadcrumbs and fresh mixed herbs, and bake for about 20 minutes in a medium to hot oven (200°C/400°F/gas mark 6).

Harvest the courgettes once they reach 10–15cm (4–6in) in length. If you keep picking, you will encourage more to form.

peppers

capsicum spp.

These tender perennials are grown as annuals in cooler climates. They are an excellent source of both vitamin C and phytochemicals, and they also contain a good quantity of vitamin A, potassium and iron. Peppers vary in 'hotness', depending on the type grown. You may well choose to grow the very hot, chilli peppers for decoration as much as for flavour; the sweet peppers, which are milder, are used in a wide range of dishes.

VARIETIES

sweet peppers 'Big Bertha': a large-fruiting green pepper, maturing to red; 'Bell Boy': a similarly large-fruiting green pepper, also maturing to red; 'Chocolate Bell': dark brownish-purple fruit; 'Purple Beauty': deep purplish-black fruit; 'Mandy': virus-resistant, green fruit, maturing to red; 'Hero': a good choice for containers as it is virus-resistant and tolerates low temperatures.
chillies 'Long Slim': attractive, slender, cayenne-type; 'Hungarian Yellow Wax': hot, yellow fruit.

CONTAINER SIZE

Plant one to each 20cm (8in) diameter pot.

CULTIVATION

Make no mistake, peppers are not the easiest crop to grow, in or out of containers. However, they are great fun and well worth a try, although insufficient sun may prevent them from ripening. You can start them off

in small seed pots or blocks indoors (three seeds to a small pot or block) about three months before the predicted last frost dates for your area. Try to make sure that they get plenty of sunshine once they germinate. When the seedlings are growing strongly, you can thin them down to the strongest in each pot (don't pull them out, simply cut them off at the stem base to prevent disturbing the roots of the remaining plant), and then harden them off (see page 20), once all danger of frost has passed, for a week before planting in their final, larger containers. Hot chilli peppers will not need as much room as sweet ones.

Pinch out the plant tops once they reach 15cm (6in) high to encourage bushy growth with lots of side shoots. Keep peppers well watered. Lack of water produces a fiery taste and possibly a bitter flavour too. Keep them sheltered from winds, and in very hot weather, provide them with partial shade. Textbooks often tell you to allow only four to six peppers per plant, but most of us are lucky to get four!

Once the fruit start swelling, apply a high-potash liquid feed once a fortnight. If the peppers are developing late in the season, move the containers indoors to a warm windowsill.

If you are growing both hot and sweet peppers, they may cross-pollinate, giving you some surprise flavours!

Aphids, red spider mite (primarily indoors), whiteflies and caterpillars can all cause problems. Spraying the leaves with water from time to time will help prevent aphids and red spider mite. Keep an eye out for pests, removing them by hand when spotted. Mosaic virus (which also attacks aubergines and cucumbers) can be a major problem, so buying virus resistant-cultivars is a good idea.

HARVESTING   Keep picking peppers and chillies to encourage new fruit to form.

vegetable pasta sauce

Peel and slice the onions finely and cook in preheated pan with the oil until just soft. Deseed and slice the peppers and chilli, and add to the onions. Cook for a few minutes, and then add the other ingredients. Cook for long enough for the ingredients to become soft, but not mushy, and the sauce to have thickened slightly (about 10 minutes). You can add black olives, capers and/or anchovies to this sauce if you wish, just before you serve it. You can also add an aubergine, cut in small cubes, just after the onions. It gives the sauce a more meaty content. Serve with plenty of grated Parmesan cheese.

2 onions

2 tbs olive oil

2 peppers

1 small chilli

6 tomatoes, skinned and quartered

1 tin tomatoes

1 tsp tomato concentrate

2 tbs mixed parsley, basil, marjoram, thyme, chopped

scant $^1/_4$pt (150ml) chicken stock

seasoning

roasted vegetables

These make an excellent accompaniment to roasted or grilled meat or fish. You can vary the vegetables and quantities according to what is in season.

Heat the oven to 220°C/425°F/gas mark 7. Peel the onions. Chop the other vegetables into quarters (or roughly 5cm/2in chunks). Brush a roasting tin with some of the olive oil and spread the vegetables on the base. Season to taste. Brush with the remaining oil, sprinkle with the breadcrumbs and herbs, and roast for approximately 30 minutes until softened and starting to char slightly. Sprinkle with flakes of Parmesan cheese.

variation
If you wish, you can add root vegetables to the dish, but remember that they take longer to cook, so put them in 15 minutes before the other ingredients.

450g (1lb) onions, peppers, tomatoes, courgettes, aubergine

3 tbs olive oil

3 tbs breadcrumbs

3 tbs mixed fresh herbs

2 tbs Parmesan cheese, flaked

seasoning

aubergines
solanum melongena

Although we are now familiar with purple-fruited aubergines, you can find white, yellow and green ones, too, and a range of curious shapes and sizes. Aubergines need warm temperatures and a long growing season to bear fruit, so if you want to try them you need to sow seed early. If you succeed in growing them, aubergines are a good source of vitamin C, iron and fibre. They are also a great talking point! If you have trouble growing them out of doors, bring the pot indoors onto a sunny window ledge. Allow roughly 20 weeks between sowing and harvesting.

Aubergines will usually crop fairly heavily if the conditions are right, but they do need shelter and sunshine to fruit well.

VARIETIES

'Long Purple': an old-fashioned favourite that has stood the test of time; 'Moneymaker': large purple fruit; 'Snowy': long white fruit; 'Kermit': green and white fruit, unusual round shape.

CONTAINER SIZE

Plant one plant in each 20cm (8in) diameter pot or three plants to a standard-sized growing bag.

CULTIVATION

Aubergine seeds can be difficult to germinate, and it helps to soak them first to soften the hard outer casing. They can take between a fortnight and three weeks to germinate. Sow three seeds to a pot in mid-spring under cover and thin to the strongest seedling when these reach 8cm (3in) in height. Harden off (see page 20) over a week or so. Aubergines need shelter from strong winds and will benefit from slight shade in very hot weather. A cloche or glass protection may be needed to encourage fruiting in colder climates. Keep them well watered. Stake the plant with a cane. You can encourage the plant to bush out more by pinching out the leading shoot once the plant reaches 30cm (12in) in height. Feed regularly with a high-potash organic fertilizer once the fruit begin to form. Should your plant produce copious quantities of fruit, reduce the number to four to encourage these to swell fully.

The main potential problems are aphids and red spider mite. Remove any aphids by hand and spray the leaves and shoots regularly with water to discourage red spider mite.

HARVESTING   Snip off any fruit regularly, with 2cm (1in) of stalk, once they reach about 10cm (4in) in size. Regular picking will encourage fruiting. Aubergines will keep in the refrigerator for up to two weeks.

'Black Knight' is a popular variety of aubergine and one that fruits well in cooler climates. As with all tender vegetables, protection will increase the likelihood of the fruit ripening.

beignets d'aubergine

These aubergine fritters are made with a very light batter. You can use the same batter to fry courgette flowers, too. Simply mix the flour with a little seasoning and enough water to make a thin cream. Then, just before using the batter, stiffly beat two egg whites and fold them into the mixture. Cut the aubergines into thin rings, dip them in the batter and fry in deep, very hot oil for a couple of minutes only. Drain on kitchen paper. Courgette flower fritters require a very brief frying time.

4 heaped tbs flour

1 large or two small aubergines

2 egg whites

seasoning

oil for frying

aubergines with goat's cheese

These make a quick, delicious lunch or supper. Slice the aubergines into 1cm (1/2in) thick rounds. Brush both sides with olive oil. Preheat a skillet and fry the aubergines on each side until just tender. Preheat the grill to the highest temperature. Spread one side of each aubergine slice with a thickish layer of the tomato paste and sprinkle with the crushed garlic. Slice the goat's cheese into rings and put one ring on each aubergine slice. Preheat the grill and grill the aubergine slices until the cheese melts. Sprinkle with basil, season to taste and serve on a bed of rocket salad.

2 aubergines

2 tbs olive oil

sun-dried tomato paste (or similar)

2 cloves garlic, finely chopped or crushed

1 goat's cheese

1 tbs torn basil leaves

seasoning

OTHER VEGETABLES

kohlrabi
brassica oleracea 'gongylodes'

This member of the cabbage family is grown for its swollen, bulb-like stem, which varies in colour from pale green to purple. There are fast- and slow-maturing varieties, the fastest taking about a month and a half to mature. The former can be sown as late as early autumn for winter supplies, otherwise sow kohlrabi seeds in mid-spring, three to a pot, thinning to one per 15cm (6in) diameter container. Unlike many other vegetables, kohlrabi is relatively drought tolerant, but will grow best if watered frequently.

turnip
brassica rapa **rapifera group**

This is a biennial whose roots are a rich source of vitamin C and a good source of vitamin A, folic acid and calcium. The white or yellow roots are cooked. Although large turnips can be slightly tasteless, the French have long enjoyed very young turnips, which suit container-growing admirably. Plant the seeds in spring and thin out to 10cm (4in) between plants once the seedlings reach 8cm (3in) tall. If you grow them successionally from spring to early summer, you will have a constant supply from summer to autumn. Use a bolt-resistant variety for later sowings and make sure you water turnips well at all times. 'Golden Ball' is a good yellow-fleshed turnip, and 'Tokyo Cross' is quick growing. Harvest once the roots are 5cm (2in) in diameter. Turnips are not particularly prone to pests and diseases, although young seedlings may be attacked by flea beetle. Protect them with cloches to prevent attacks.

artichoke, globe
cynara cardunculus

Whether or not you choose to eat its curiously armadillo-like flower buds, the artichoke makes a handsome feature plant in its own right, with its large silvery leaves and attractive blue flowers. It will benefit from a large container, at least 25cm (10in) in diameter. It is probably best to grow artichokes by purchasing a container-grown plant or dividing an existing plant; otherwise, you will have to wait two years for the flower buds to form. For culinary purposes, harvest the flower buds in midsummer, while they are still young, cutting them from the main plant just below the base of the bud with a sharp knife. Keep picking to encourage further production.

The nutty, potato-like root is full of flavour and a valuable source of vitamin B. Jerusalem artichokes are easy and quick to grow, but are also very large. Grow them as you would potatoes, in a deepish barrel, from mature artichoke roots cut into pieces and planted 8cm (3in) deep. The plants will grow to 1.8m (6ft) tall and will make an excellent windbreak for other more tender plants. Harvest the roots in autumn. Jerusalem artichokes are pest and disease free. The downside, however, is that they can cause a considerable amount of gas in the stomach!

You can make an excellent mashed potatoes by cooking both Jersualem artichokes and potatoes together until tender and then mashing them with a good dollop of butter and a generous quantity of single cream. Chop in a tablespoonful of parsley, and season with pepper and salt. Jerusalem artichokes also make excellent soup (see basic soup recipe on page 139).

artichoke, jerusalem
helianthus tuberosus

FAR LEFT   Turnips are delicious if harvested young and small.

LEFT   Artichokes should also be picked when young for the best flavour and texture. 'Green Globe' shown here is a popular and useful variety.

fruit

soft fruit · bush fruit · tree fruit · other fruit

strawberries

fragaria x ananassa

Although we often think of strawberries as having a short season, lasting for just a few weeks in midsummer, it is possible, with a little forethought and ingenuity, to enjoy a much longer strawberry season. There are several varieties of strawberry, known as remontant or perpetual, which fruit later than usual, and continue to do so until late autumn. You can also force summer-fruiting strawberries to ripen earlier in the season by covering them with a plastic cloche.

RIGHT　'Elsanta' is a good choice for a hanging basket, with abundant crops of small, sweet fruit.

FAR RIGHT　A purpose-made strawberry pot maximizes space.

OPPOSITE　'Gorella' strawberries growing in individual terracotta pots on wooden staging on a narrow balcony.

Strawberries grow very well in pots and tubs of all kinds. Modern strawberry production favours growing bags on raised tables. Grown this way, they are less prone to attacks by slugs and vine weevils. You can also buy purpose-made strawberry pots, with planting pockets up the sides of the pot, or you can create one yourself out of a barrel. Drill holes roughly 8cm (3in) in diameter up the sides, staggering them around the barrel, roughly 40cm (6in) apart. Originating in woodland conditions, strawberries, unlike many other fruit, will tolerate part shade but they fruit much better in full sun. After a couple of years, the plants will be exhausted, but you can pot up the runners that form each year to increase your stock.

VARIETIES

There is a wide range to choose from, from early and mid-season to late-autumn-fruiting crops, as well as the smaller alpine forms of strawberry (*F. vesca*), which make up for the lack of size with exceptionally sweet, full-flavoured fruit. Among the best of the early and mid-season strawberries are 'Florence', 'Elsanta', 'Elvira' and 'Royal Sovereign'.

Late-fruiting types include 'Gorella' and 'Cambridge Late Pine'. Remontant (or perpetual) varieties, which fruit for a much longer season include the French variety, 'Mara des Bois', which has the flavour of a woodland strawberry with the size of a cultivated one and is an extremely heavy cropper.

CONTAINER SIZE

You can grow strawberries in small pots (15cm/6in in diameter) – a single plant will produce up to 500g (1lb) of strawberries – one plant to each pot. Special strawberry planters allow you to grow up to 20 plants in each pot, making good use of the available space.

CULTIVATION

Buy young strawberry plants in late summer and plant them up in early autumn. Unless you plan to devote a lot of space to strawberries, it is probably better to plant several plants that fruit at the same time. Make sure that the plants are well watered at all times. If you grow them in a strawberry planter, take care that the lowest plants get an adequate water supply. Feed with an organic fertilizer from flowering onwards. Once the fruits start to swell, watch out for slugs and snails (although these tend to be less of a problem with container-grown plants) and remove them. In late summer remove any offshoots (runners) and plant them up in separate pots to increase your stock of strawberries.

Birds are the greatest problem and you may need to net your strawberry containers.

HARVESTING

Pick the fruits as soon as they redden. Strawberries do not keep well, nor do they freeze well. Eat them the day they are picked.

STRAWBERRIES FOR THE TABLE

You can use strawberries either as the main ingredient for a dessert or, if you have very few, as a decoration. They make a marvellous accompaniment to fresh lemon tart (made using the recipe for plum tart on page 121, but substituting lemons for the plums; you will need the rind and juice of two fresh lemons). Strawberry ice cream is equally delicious. Use the ice cream recipe on page 106, substituting strawberries for the main ingredient.

strawberry mille-feuilles

Cut the filo pasty into neat rectangles about 8cm x 4cm (3in x 1½in) in size and place on a greased baking sheet. Cook in a very hot oven (or as directed on the packet) until crisp and golden. Remove and cool on a wire rack. Beat the cream until thick. Slice the strawberries and layer the strawberries with the cream between the sheets of filo pastry. Dust the tops of the slices with icing sugar and garnish each one with half a strawberry and a sprig of mint.

100g (4oz) filo pastry (ready-made)
300ml (½pt) double cream
450g (1lb) strawberries
icing sugar and mint sprigs to garnish

strawberries and lemon syllabub

The combination of **strawberries** with lemon always works well. You only need a few strawberries for this. If you wish, you can substitute peaches for the strawberries.

Halve the strawberries and divide them evenly among four glasses, reserving four for decoration. Whip the cream, adding the lemon juice and rind, white wine and sugar gradually to prevent curdling. Spoon the mixture over the strawberries and decorate with a single strawberry and a sprinkling of brown sugar. Chill well before serving.

225g (8oz) strawberries, washed and hulled
300ml (½pt) double cream
juice and rind of 2 small lemons
½ glass sweet white wine
50g (2oz) caster sugar

B U S H   F R U I T

There are several types of bush fruit, all of which will do well in containers. You can choose from brambles (*Rosaceae* family), such as raspberries and blackberries, or currants and gooseberries (*Grossulariaceae* family). There are hybridized raspberries and blackberries and hybridized currants and gooseberries, too. Loganberries are a cross between raspberries and blackberries, with exceptionally large, wine-coloured fruit, while jostaberries, for example, are a hybrid between gooseberries and blackcurrants, with particularly large black fruits.

Even if you do not manage to get a very large crop from a single bush, there is nothing to stop you growing several different types and then using the mixed fruit in various desserts – summer pudding, fruit pudding or ice creams, for example – or for making a mixed fruit jam.

You will need to provide a suitable support framework for raspberries and blackberries, both of which are best grown against a sunny wall. Use a simple trellis system of posts and wires. The greatest yield of fruit will be obtained if you train the new canes horizontally along the wires, tying them in with string or twist ties.

If you wish, you can train your gooseberry bushes into small standards by removing the lower sideshoots, to create a mop-head of foliage (and fruit) at the top.

You can get surprisingly good yields from a single fruit bush if you feed the plants with a potash-based fertilizer in early spring. A mulch of your own compost or straw around the base of the plant will help to retain moisture and, in the case of compost, feed the plants at the same time.

RIGHT Young 'Invicta' gooseberries (right) and 'Laxton's Giant' blackcurrants (far right).

gooseberries

ribes uva-crispa

There are two kinds of gooseberry – the dessert gooseberry with large golden or reddish fruits and the small-fruited culinary gooseberry. Both are grown in the same way, but the culinary gooseberries are more heat-tolerant and mildew-resistant. If you wish, you can grow gooseberry bushes as half-standards with a couple of feet of clear stem and underplant them with herbs.

VARIETIES

dessert gooseberries 'Early Sulphur', 'Langley Gage' and 'Leveller' (all yellow); 'Poorman' and 'Clark' (red).
culinary gooseberries 'Careless'; 'Jubilee'; 'Invicta'.

CONTAINER SIZE

Plant in a container at least 30cm (12in) in diameter.

CULTIVATION

Plant young gooseberry bushes in autumn. A sunny site will produce the best crop, but they will cope with partial shade. They prefer lower amounts of nitrogen and plenty of potassium and magnesium. Mulching the container with gravel or straw after planting will help to conserve moisture. Feed with a high-potash fertilizer in early spring. Once the fruit sets, you need to water regularly. If you let the compost dry out and then water copiously, the fruit may burst. Prune after fruiting, taking lateral shoots back to three to five leaves but leaving leaders unpruned, and prune to an outward-facing bud. Aphids and mildews are the main problems. Remove aphids by hand and use sulphur to control mildews.

HARVEST

Pick early gooseberries for jams or compotes, and later ones for fully ripe dessert gooseberries.

Dessert gooseberries, which are larger and sweeter than the culinary forms, are eaten raw. Those shown here are 'Langley Gage'.

currants

ribes nigrum (blackcurrants)*, r. rubrum* (white- and redcurrants)

Currants do well in containers and are relatively easy to grow and maintain. They will grow to about 1.5m (5ft) tall, bearing white, red, black or gold currants, according to the type. Although currants are self-fertile, many cultivars benefit from cross-pollination, so it pays to grow more than one bush if you can. Unlike gooseberries, they like plenty of nitrogen, so feed them accordingly. With good plant management, you should obtain a good yield off just one plant, even up to 4.5kg (10lb) per bush. Jostaberries (a cross between gooseberries and blackcurrants) crop slightly less heavily.

VARIETIES

blackcurrants 'Ben Sarek': a dwarf variety with lots of fruit; 'Laxton's Giant': particularly large, sweet fruits.
redcurrants 'Red Lake' and 'Malling Redstart': both heavy fruiting.
whitecurrants 'White Versailles': good all rounder; 'White Imperial': good flavour.

CONTAINER SIZE

A 30cm (12in) diameter container is best, although, as they are fairly shallow rooted, you could grow them in a growing bag.

CULTIVATION

Plant currant bushes in autumn or winter. Blackcurrants need to be planted deeper than redcurrants – with the uppermost roots about 8cm (3in) below the surface. The roots of redcurrants can be about 2.5cm

(1in) below the surface of the compost. Mulching the surface after planting with gravel or chipped bark will help to retain moisture. Apply high-nitrogen organic fertilizer at the start of the growing season and keep the soil moist. Cut back the leading shoots by roughly half after planting and trim the lateral shoots to a couple of buds, making the cuts above downward- and outward-facing buds. Prune lightly in subsequent years to keep an open-shaped bush. Alternatively, you can grow red- and whitecurrants as cordons by removing all but one of the leaders and then training this up a stake. Aphids and mildew can be problems on currants.

Currants will be ready for picking from midsummer onwards, depending on the cultivar. When you harvest them, remove a whole fruit cluster rather than the individual fruits. Currants do not keep well once picked, but they freeze extremely well.

HARVESTING

Whitecurrants have excellent flavour but tend to crop less heavily than the more ubiquitous blackcurrants.

raspberries

rubus idaea

There are two fruiting seasons for raspberries, summer and autumn, so if you choose the right varieties you can extend the raspberry season. You can also grow raspberry/blackberry hybrids with names like tayberry, worcesterberry, boysenberry and loganberry – the last being the most commonly known.

VARIETIES

There are early-, mid- and late-summer raspberries, and autumn-fruiting ones as well.

summer fruiting 'Boyne': early-season, red fruits; 'Algonquin': mid-season, red fruits; 'Haida': late-season, red fruits.

autumn fruiting 'Autumn Bliss': early autumn, large fruits; 'Ruby': late autumn, very large fruits.

CONTAINER SIZE

Plant two or three plants in a container about 30cm (12in) across. For a good crop, have at least two such containers.

CULTIVATION

Plant young raspberry plants in late autumn or early spring in a fairly alkaline growing medium and set any bare-root plants about 5cm (2in) deeper than they were in the nursery. Let the roots spread out. Cut off the canes to just above ground level after planting, as this will help prevent diseases. Give raspberries a good dose of compost or organic fertilizer in early spring. Keep well watered during the growing season. Provide a support system of trellising. Summer-fruiting raspberries are pruned after fruiting in early autumn by cutting off fruiting canes to ground level; autumn-fruiting canes are pruned in early spring. Although they can fall prey to pests and diseases, they are usually easy to grow. If raspberry beetle is a problem spray with derris. Viruses cause stunting of the plant so buy virus-resistant cultivars or certified stock. Anthracnose causes blackish blotches on leaves and fruit. Aphids spread diseases, so spray with insecticidal soap.

Pick raspberries as they ripen. Picking will help encourage more raspberries to form but don't pick while they are wet. Put them into the refrigerator immediately after picking – they do not keep well.

BELOW LEFT A loganberry, which is a cross between a raspberry and a blackberry.

BELOW RIGHT 'Autumn Bliss', a heavy-cropping late-fruiting raspberry.

HARVESTING

gooseberry and elderflower fool

450g (1lb) gooseberries
100g (4oz) caster sugar
10 elderflower heads
juice of 1 lemon and half of rind
300ml (1/2pt) double cream
sprigs of mint to decorate

Stew the gooseberries in a pan with a few tablespoonsful of water. Allow them to simmer until soft. Add the sugar and dissolve it over the heat, stirring. Wash the elderflower heads and wrap them in muslin, tied up like a giant teabag. Drop the elderflower bag into the mixture and add the lemon juice and rind. Cook for a further 5 minutes or so, squashing the elderflowers down with the back of the spoon. Remove the bag and sieve the gooseberries into a bowl. Fold in the cream gently. Pour into individual dishes, decorate with mint and chill for an hour or so before serving.

raspberry crème brûlée

150g (6oz) raspberries
300ml (1/2pt) double cream
3 tbs of caster sugar
brown sugar to cover

Although raspberries are particularly good as a base for this crème brûlée, you could use other tart fresh fruit in season. Blackcurrants would be a good substitute, but unless they are very ripe you will need to stew them lightly first with some sugar.

Divide the fruit into four ramekins. Beat the double cream until it thickens, but is not solid. Stir in the sugar. Pour over the raspberries and leave to chill in the refrigerator for an hour or so. Just before serving, heat the grill to the highest temperature, sprinkle the demerara sugar on top of the ramekins to make a thinnish crust, and set under the grill until the crust bubbles and browns. Allow to cool and serve.

blackcurrant ice cream

450g (1lb) blackcurrants
100g (4oz) caster sugar
300ml (1/2pt) double cream
1 egg white

If you have an ice cream maker, it will produce the best results. Other fruit can be used in place of the blackcurrants – strawberries or blueberries, for example.

Stew the blackcurrants lightly for 3–4 minutes with the sugar and a couple of tablespoonsful of water. Allow to cool. Lightly whip the cream and fold into the fruit. Pour into a polythene container and partially freeze. Stir. Whisk the egg white until stiff and fold into the mixture. Freeze again until the mixture is fully frozen. Serve with macaroons or almond biscuits.

fruit coulis

You can make a fresh fruit sauce out of strawberries, raspberries or currants. Wash and hull the fruit. Blend with the sugar and lemon juice in a blender. Sieve if the fruit has pips. Pour into a freezer bag or container and freeze. Serve chilled (allow a couple of hours for it to unfreeze) with ice cream or Greek yoghourt, for example.

225g (8oz) of fresh fruit (such as blackcurrants, raspberries or blackberries, or a mixture)

75g (3oz) sugar

juice of 1 lemon

red fruit compote

Hull or stone and wash whatever red fruit you have grown: raspberries, currants, strawberries, plums and cherries. Add enough brown sugar to sweeten, together with the lemon zest and juice. Add just enough water to cover and simmer gently until just tender. Serve warm with crème fraîche.

450g (1lb) whatever soft red fruit you have grown

3 tbs brown sugar

rind and juice of 1 lemon

red fruit salad with kirsch

Make a light syrup with the caster sugar and 150ml (¼pt) water. Allow to cool. Wash the fruit, slice the strawberries and grapes in half, and top and tail the currants. Pour the kirsch and the syrup over the fruit. Decorate with a sprig of mint.

450g (1lb) mixed red fruit: strawberries, raspberries, blackcurrants, blueberries or black grapes

2 tbs caster sugar

liqueur glass of kirsch

sprig of mint

g r a p e s
vitis vinifera

A grape vine is well worth growing, even in colder climates, if only for the attractive canopy of foliage. However, it should be possible to get a crop of dessert grapes, even if the chance of wine-making eludes you, as wine grapes require a high concentration of sugar, which occurs only if there is a long, hot summer. Grape vines will not fruit until they are three years old, so if you buy a young plant, you have a bit of a wait ahead of you before you can pick your first bunch of grapes.

VARIETIES

The most commonly grown wine grape are cultivars of *Vitis vinifera,* which are grown on US rootstock after phylloxera, an aphid, caused widespread damage in Europe. *Vitis* 'Brandt' is a commonly grown ornamental and edible grape vine, which produces small, black grapes; it is very vigorous and makes useful wall cover. 'Müller-Thurgau' is a popular wine-making grape that produces a riesling-type wine.

CONTAINER SIZE

A good-sized half-barrel or a Versailles tub is probably the best option for a grape vine.

CULTIVATION

Plant a grape vine in autumn or spring. Position it against a west- or south-facing wall for maximum sunshine. You will need to train it across a trellis system of stakes and wires. Pruning a grape vine correctly is essential for fruit production, and there are two principal systems: cordon and the Guyot method. Although the latter produces maximum

Grapes do very well in containers, with the advantage that you can move the pot into a sunny position as the fruit starts to ripen.

fruit yield, for amateur growers the cordon method is easier. For this, you will need to stake the leading shoot to a stout cane and then train the lateral shoots, alternately right and left, to horizontal wires held against the wall and fence. In the first two years, in spring and summer, cut the lateral shoots back to three leaves. In the autumn of the second year shorten the leading shoot by half of the new growth and cut the laterals back to within 2.5cm (1in) of the leading shoot. Then in the third and subsequent years, when the flowers appear, cut the lateral shoots back to two leaves beyond the flowers, and cut back any shoots off the main laterals to just one leaf, the aim being to keep just one bunch of grapes to each fruiting spur. As the vine develops, you can increase this in future years to two to three bunches on each fruiting spur. Once the vine has reached the required height, snip off the leading shoot.

From spring to autumn feed regularly with a high-potash organic fertilizer to encourage fruiting. Remove leaves that cover trusses to expose the fruit to more sunlight. Water regularly throughout, and when the grapes start to ripen net them to protect them from birds.

The most common problems are scale insects, bird damage and mildews and moulds.

HARVESTING

Depending on the type grown, grapes are normally harvested in early to mid-autumn. Generally, they are fully ripe once the stem has started to turn slightly brown. The bunch of grapes is cut off the vine with a 5cm (2in) stem.

GRAPES FOR THE TABLE

Nothing is more delicious than a bunch of home-grown grapes. Serve them with a salty cheese, on a bed of vine leaves, for dessert.

frosted grapes and other fruit and flowers

As a decoration for other desserts, you can frost individual fruits and edible flowers by painting each one with beaten egg white, and then dipping it in sifted caster sugar, holding the fruit or flower with tweezers. Dry them on a sheet of baking parchment. You can store them for a day or two between sheets of parchment in an airtight container.

grapes, cherries, strawberries, currants, rose petals, pansies

1 egg white, beaten

caster sugar

grape and pear salad

Peel, core and halve the pears. Spread the outer surface of the pears with cream cheese, and cover with rows of halved grapes, arranged lengthways until each pear is fully covered. Arrange the pear halves on a bed of lettuce and serve with cold chicken or gammon.

3 pears

100g (4oz) cream cheese

small bunch of grapes

1/2 lettuce

vine leaves filled with cheese

Wash and dry the vine leaves, then blanch in boiling water for 2 minutes. Dry them again and place one cheese in the centre of each leaf. Make a parcel of each one, wrapping it with raffia. Place on a baking sheet, pour the olive oil over the parcels, and cook in a preheated oven (220°C/ 425°F/gas mark 7) for 10 minutes or so, or until the cheese has started to melt. Serve decorated with halved tomatoes.

6 vine leaves

6 small goat's cheeses with creamy flavour

3 tbs olive oil

12 cherry tomatoes

TREE FRUIT

You can grow all kinds of tree fruit very successfully in containers, particularly the dwarf varieties that are now available, bred specifically for growing in limited space. All apple trees are propagated by grafting small pieces of the cultivar in question onto a basic rootstock. Those for container growing have an M27 rootstock, which produces a tree roughly 15 per cent of the full size. Whereas a standard tree will reach about 9m (30ft) and will not bear fruit for at least six years, these smaller trees will only reach about 1.5m (5ft) and will bear fruit in half the time or even less. You can also buy minarette trees, which are ideal for containers. They are trained to a single tall stem and fruit well, although not as copiously as other types of tree.

Remember that many fruit trees (particularly apples, pears and some plums) require a suitable partner tree – one that blooms at roughly the same time – for pollination purposes, although a few varieties of plum are self-fertile.

If your fruit trees fail to produce fruit, check the nutrient and mineral content of the growing medium. Fruit needs high levels of potassium and also calcium and boron. Too much nitrogen will lead to a lot of leaf but is not conducive to fruiting. A soil-test kit will indicate any nutrient deficiencies. A foliar feed using seaweed extract, and a spoonful or two of gypsum should improve matters. Mulching the surface of the container will help to retain moisture.

All fruit trees need adequate amounts of sunlight to set fruit. Sound staking helps to prevent wind rock. Remember when planting that the graft unions of the cultivar to the rootstock (the knobbly bulge on the

stem) should be about 5cm (2in) above the level of the growing medium otherwise suckers may form.

When pruning fruit trees, bear in mind that they generally benefit from an open structure that allows air to circulate around the branches, so the aim is to develop a central leading shoot with widely spaced lateral branches that will bear the fruits on their sideshoots. Prune apples and pears in early spring and stone fruits after the buds form.

If you wish, you can train a container-grown tree into a fan, espalier or cordon shape. With an espalier, the branches are trained at right angles either side of the main leader; in a fan the branches are at a 45 degree angle to the main leader, and with cordons the leader itself is at a 45 degree angle. These training systems are useful when growing fruit trees against a wall or fence, as they take up little room while allowing the maximum sunshine to reach the fruit so that it ripens successfully.

Should you be so lucky as to have trees that bear too much fruit, it is a good idea to thin them out; otherwise the weight of the fruit may damage the branches. (Bear in mind that the first few years of any new fruit tree are lean, and do not expect buckets full of fruit until several years later.) Large fruits can be thinned to about 15cm (6in) apart and small fruits to about 8cm (3in) apart.

All fruit trees are subject to a wide range of pests and diseases, making them more difficult to grow than most vegetables, herbs and flowers. You can help increase resistance to attack by ensuring that plants are as healthy as possible, and kept stress-free through regular and appropriate feeding and watering. If you net trees, you will ensure that the birds, at least, do not get the crop before you do. Grease bands around the trunk will help to prevent some pests. For others there is no form of organic control, except extreme watchfulness, removing pests by hand and removing diseased shoots and branches when first sighted. Chemical controls for most diseases do exist, but you have to weigh up the pros and cons of using them.

Plums are heavy-cropping fruit (those shown left are 'Black Star'). The best to grow in containers are those with a dwarfing rootstock.

apples

malus domestica

Apples are the most popular fruits, and there is a wide range of cultivars bearing distinctly different types of apple, from sour cookers to sweet dessert apples. Some trees have been grafted to produce a family tree with three different apples on one rootstock. Some apple cultivars bear their fruit on spurs (side shoots of laterals) while others bear them on the tips of the branches. You will need to know which type you are dealing with in order to prune it properly. Instructions are normally given on the label of the fruit tree when you purchase it.

CULTIVARS
'Grenadier': soft, sour cooking apple; 'Cox's Orange Pippin': crisp, sweet dessert apple that keeps well; 'Worcester Pearmain': soft, sweet dessert apple. The above will all pollinate each other.

CONTAINER SIZE
At least 60cm (24in) across and 60cm (24in) deep.

CULTIVATION
Plant and stake securely in autumn or early spring and cut the main shoot and the laterals back to one-third, and any sideshoots back to four buds. Mulch the surface of the container to help retain moisture and make sure the container does not dry out after the buds form. Foliar feeding with seaweed extract will help to promote fruiting.

HARVESTING
Pick fruit from mid-autumn to early winter, according to the variety. If you store apples, put them on racks in a cool, dry place and so that they do not touch each other. Alternatively, slice them and freeze them.

Apples are harvested from
late summer to mid-autumn,
depending on the variety.
'Sunset', left, is an early
autumn dessert apple.

pears

pyrus communis

Pears lend themselves to all kinds of culinary treats. The trees are relatively easy to grow, and more resistant to pest and diseases than many fruit trees although frosts may damage flowers. Dwarf pears suitable for containers are grafted onto various rootstocks.

VARIETIES

As with other fruit trees, you will need to grow more than one cultivar of an appropriate type to ensure pollination takes place and fruit sets (unless more than one cultivar is grafted on). 'Conference': long pear with good flavour; relatively trouble free. 'Comice': sweet dessert pear.

CONTAINER SIZE

At least 45cm (18in) in diameter and depth; re-pot to a container 60cm (24in) or more in diameter in a couple of years' time.

CULTIVATION

Plant and stake securely in late autumn or early spring in a sunny, sheltered spot. Ensure that the growing medium has a pH of around 6.5. Pears need boron and manganese to fruit well, so if your tree fails to bear fruit check the condition of the growing medium by doing a soil test. Make sure that the surface of the growing medium is well mulched with gravel, straw or compost as pears are susceptible to water loss. Dry conditions can cause the crop to abort completely. Prune pears as little as possible, to avoid diseases entering through the pruning cuts, but where possible keep the structure of the tree open.

HARVESTING

Early pears will be ready from late summer, later varieties from mid-autumn. If you pick pears while they are hard, they will ripen indoors.

Pear form and colour can be
vary varied, from the long,
slender, green 'Conference'
pears to this golden,
rounded 'Onward' variety.

OTHER FRUIT

figs
ficus carica

A fig tree is worth growing for its singularly beautiful, hand-shaped foliage, regardless of whether it produces its green (try 'White Marseilles') or purple-brown (try 'Brown Turkey') fruit, which are a valuable source of calcium. As the roots prefer to be restricted, a container is the ideal home for a fig tree. You may need to pot it on after a few years. Figs are generally low-maintenance plants and are trouble free. Net the fruit, however, if you do not want the birds to take it first.

cherries
prunus avium, p. cerasus

You can choose from sweet (*P. avium)* or sour cherries (*P. cerasus)*. The latter are easier to grow, hardier and self-fertile. Although some new varieties of sweet cherry are self-fertile, they generally need a compatible pollinator to set fruit (you need to check the label to ensure you choose one that is compatible). Alternatively, you can buy a tree with two cultivars grafted onto it. Cherries are an excellent source of vitamins C, A and B2. The flesh of cherries can be purple, red or yellow. Gisela 5 rootstock produces small trees suitable for containers. Of the varieties, choose 'Morello', the best-known sour cherry, or 'Stella', a self-fertile sweet cherry. Plant up in a container at least 45cm (18in) in diameter and depth; repot to a container 60cm (24in) in diameter in two years' time. Cherries will fruit in partial shade, but you will get the largest crop in full sun. Mulch well to prevent moisture loss and feed with organic fertilizer regularly from spring onwards. Water cherries thoroughly and consistently once they start to set fruit, otherwise the fruit may crack from over-watering or shrivel from under-watering. Prune cherries in late spring or in summer after fruiting to encourage formation of the next year's crop. Do not prune in autumn or winter as this may encourage silver leaf disease. Reduce the number of laterals on each main shoot to two, and cut back the side growth to three or four buds. Net the crop to protect it from the birds.

Plums, and their close cousins, damsons (*P. insititia*), are relatively hardy and largely self-fertile, but some will not stand hard winters and most will crop better if a suitable pollinator is grown nearby or grafted onto the same stock. Plums, which can be golden- or purple-fleshed, are rich in vitamins C and A. You can also find hybrids of cherries and plums. Pixy is a dwarf rootstock onto which various cultivars are grafted, making them useful for container growing. Choose disease-resistant cultivars wherever possible. 'Crimson' is resistant to many diseases; 'Belle de Louvin' has purple fruits and is self fertile; 'Opal' is a self-fertile early plum. Plant and stake a young plum tree in a container at least 45cm (18in) in diameter and depth; re-pot to a container 60cm (24in) in diameter two years' later. Site the container in a sheltered position in a sunny spot. The fruit is borne on spurs in the centre of the tree, so you need to prune to allow in as much sunlight as possible, removing old wood and leaving fruiting inner spurs, in either late autumn or early spring. Mulch the surface of the container with an organic mulch to prevent moisture loss and make sure that the plums are kept well watered in the growing season. If the tree is cropping very heavily thin the fruit. Net the tree to prevent birds from taking the crop. Handle plums as little as possible, and leave the stalk on when picking.

plums
prunus domestica

Blueberries are hardy perennials that require acid conditions (with a pH level of 4 to 5.5). Container growing is therefore ideal if you live in an area with chalky soil as you can control the acidity of the growing medium by using ericaceous compost mixed with an equal quantity of grit (to encourage free drainage). Blueberries must be fed with a fertilizer that contains no lime or calcium and should ideally be watered with rainwater in hard water areas. Mulch the surface of the container with bark chippings to retain moisture. Blueberries need little pruning, but in the second or third year, prune to remove roughly a quarter of the old wood. They can be either mid- or late-season fruiting. 'Bluecrop' is generally regarded as a good mid-season variety. They are relatively trouble free.

blueberries
vaccinium spp.

apple and apricot compote

350g (12oz) apples and apricots (the latter can be fresh or dried and soaked)

juice and rind of 1 lemon

25g (1oz) butter

150ml (¹/4pt) water

75g (3oz) caster sugar

2 cinnamon sticks

This makes a rich compote which goes very well with ice cream or Greek yoghourt. The addition of a small quantity of butter gives it more flavour amd a creamier texture. You can make a very good plain apple sauce the same way, with a little lemon juice and grated rind, but using less water.

Slice the apples and halve the apricots and put them in the pan with the lemon juice and rind and the butter. Allow to sweat in the butter for a few minutes, then add the water, sugar and cinnamon. Simmer gently for l5 minutes or until the fruit is just tender.

apple fritters

3 large tart apples

150ml (¹/4pt) pancake batter (see page 39)

vegetable oil

3 tbs caster sugar

This recipe uses the shallow-frying method. You could equally use the deep-frying method for the aubergine beignets, coating the apple slices with the beignet batter (see page 89). In either case, peel and core the apples and slice into rings, roughly 2cm (³/4in) thick. Dip the apples in the batter and add to the preheated pan of oil. Fry until the batter is crisp and the apples soft. Dredge with caster sugar and serve.

grilled plums with mascarpone

12 plums

5 heaped tbs mascarpone

4 tbs vanilla-flavoured brown sugar

sprig of mint to decorate

This is adapted from Nigel Slater's recipe in *Real Food*. You could use ripe peaches instead, but the tartness of the plums goes particularly well with the sweetness of the mascarpone. If the plums are not fully ripe, put them on a baking tray, and bake them whole in a moderate oven for about 20 minutes to soften them.

Cut the plums in half and remove the stones. Put them, cut-side up, on tinfoil on a grill pan. Cover with mascarpone. Sprinkle liberally with vanilla-flavoured sugar. Grill under a very hot grill for a few minutes until the sugar caramelizes. Allow to cool so that the sugar forms a hard crust and serve with a dollop of good-quality vanilla ice cream. Decorate each portion with a sprig of mint.

plum tart

You can make this fruit tart with whatever fruit you have available: cherries or gooseberries would be equally as good as plums. If the fruit is not particularly ripe or sweet, then stew it lightly first. Roll out the pastry and line a 20cm (8in) flan tin (or individual tartlet tins if you prefer). Prick the pastry and cover with dried beans. Bake in a moderate oven (180°C/350°C/gas mark 4) for 20 minutes. Allow to cool. Spread the fruit over the pastry base. Then beat together the eggs, sugar, lemon rind and cream and pour over the fruit. Cook in a moderate oven until just firm to the touch (about 25 minutes).

1 packet frozen shortcrust pastry

350g (12oz) fruit – plums, gooseberries or cherries

3 eggs

75g (3oz) caster sugar

rind of lemon, grated

300ml (1/2pt) double cream

pears in red wine

Peel the pears but leave the stalks on. Slice across the bottom of each to make a firm base and put the pears tail-end-up in a small saucepan with 150ml (1/4pt) of red wine and a similar quantity of water. Add the other ingredients and poach gently for 20 minutes or so, with the lid on, until the pears are just tender. Serve in individual ramekins with the sauce.

450g (1lb) ripe pears

150ml (1/4pt) red wine

3tbs brown sugar

grated rind of lemon

grated nutmeg

stick of cinnamon

herbs and edible flowers

culinary herbs add zest to vegetable dishes; edible flowers help salads and drinks to sparkle

HERBS

Without doubt, herbs are the best edible plants to grow in containers. They are well suited to the size, and provided you have a reasonably sunny place for them, you will be rewarded with some wonderful flavours and great benefits to your general wellbeing, and often to your digestion, too. The seeds of herbs such as dill and coriander help the digestion of carbohydrates, while the green herbs – parsley, thyme and marjoram – appear to help metabolize fats and oils, and are widely used with fried or fatty food. Although there is no reason why you should not experiment with some of the more unusual herbs, the commonly used culinary herbs are a good place to start.

Everyone develops particular favourites, but basil and parsley are the staple herbs used in most Western cooking, with coriander the most popular addition to Eastern dishes. Coriander is more difficult to grow in temperate climates than the other two. Although parsley is hardy, basil is tender and can be grown only as an annual in summer, although the bush form of basil is half-hardy and will often survive the winter in town centres, which are usually warmer than outlying areas.

Because most herbs will do just as well on a window ledge as anywhere else, if this is the only space you have available, do grow them, along with a few of the smaller vegetables, such as lettuces, radishes and rocket, and perhaps even some miniature vegetables, such as baby carrots or baby beetroot.

OPPOSITE   Marjoram (right) and parsley (far right) are easy-to-grow herbs.

chives
allium schoenoprasum

Chives are hardy bulbous perennials, and a member of the onion family. They grow to 23cm (8in) tall, with long, slender leaves and small purple or mauve bell-shaped flowers borne in umbels in summer. 'Forescate' is slightly larger, growing to 45cm (18in) tall.

purpose

The leaves are chopped for use in salads, in egg dishes and as decoration for other dishes, such as grilled meat or fish. The characteristic 'oniony' smell is caused by sulphur compounds, which are thought to benefit the circulation and the digestive system.

cultivation

Grow chives in small containers or window boxes. Sow the seed in spring, thinning to one plant per 15cm (6in) pot in a sunny spot. Plants can be susceptible to downy mildew or attacks from onion fly, but they are generally fairly tough and pest and disease resistant.

dill
anethum graveolens

Dill is a hardy perennial and an attractive member of the umbellifer family, with branching flowerheads and feathery leaves. It does best in sun and will grow to about 1.2m (4ft) tall, but there is a cultivar called 'Fernleaf' which is much smaller (about 45cm/18in).

purpose

The prime value of dill in nutritional terms is to aid digestion and it helps dispel wind. (It was the main ingredient in the gripe water I was given as a child.) The leaves, seeds and oil are all used for culinary purposes.

cultivation

Sow the seed in spring, thinning the plants to one per 15cm (6in) pot or plant three to a 30cm (12in) pot. Sow at intervals if you want a quantity of dill leaves or seeds. Gather the leaves in late spring or summer, and the seeds in late summer.

coriander
coriandrum sativum

A tender perennial, coriander is grown in cold climates as a annual. It grows to about 30cm (12in) high and will flourish in partial shade.

purpose

The leaves, seeds and oil are all used in cooking, and it has pronounced antibacterial properties. The leaves and seeds are widely used in Oriental cooking, as an aid to digestion as well as a flavouring.

cultivation

Sow the seed in spring and thin to three plants per 15cm (6in) pot. Harvest the leaves in early summer and the seeds in late summer. Coriander has a tendency to bolt in hot weather, so move the pots to a more shady position if temperatures rise and keep the pots well watered.

This half-hardy tree will grow to 7m (23ft) or more in the wild, but it is slow growing and is ideally suited to containers. The evergreen leaves are dark green, oval and glossy. In spring established bay trees bear clusters of small yellow flowers.

bay
laurus nobilis

purpose

The leaves are highly aromatic and add flavour to soups and stews, either fresh or dried, usually in a bouquet garni of other herbs. Bay is reputed to have strong antiseptic properties and also aids digestion.

cultivation

Grow from cuttings taken in summer. Bay prefers sun but will grow in partial shade. Prune it in late summer. It can be trained into topiary shapes, such as simple balls or pyramids, or grown as a clear-stemmed standard tree. The clippings can be dried for winter use in the kitchen. Bay suffers from scale insect attacks, which manifest themselves with curled, blotched leaves. Remove any affected leaves at the very first signs and spray the bush with insecticidal soap as a deterrent.

BELOW (LEFT TO RIGHT) The small pinkish-mauve flowerhead of chives, the umbelliferous flowers of dill (*Anethum graveolens* 'Dukat') and the aromatic evergreen leaves of bay.

mint
mentha spp.

There are many species and varieties of mint, a hardy perennial. The best known are spearmint (*Mentha spicata*) and peppermint (*M.* x *piperata*) which are widely used commercially. Plants grow to about 30cm (12in) or more and the leaves are smallish and mid-green. In cooking, mint adds a pleasant, slightly astringent flavour to vegetable dishes, such as potatoes and peas. Apple mint (*M. suaveolens*) has slightly hairier leaves than the more commonly grown spearmint and a good, fruity flavour.

purpose

The volatile oil, menthol, has long been used as an antiseptic and decongestant. Crushed mint leaves steeped in water make a good insect repellent when the liquid is used as a spray.

BELOW The slightly coarse-textured leaves of mint (below) and the smooth, soft, green leaves of basil (below right).

cultivation

Mint is invasive and tends to spread if grown in the garden but containers are the ideal way to keep plants under control. Mint prefers damp, slightly shady conditions. Grow it from runners collected from other mint plants or propagate from seed sown in spring.

basil
ocimum basilicum

This is the cook's delight. There are more than 150 varieties of basil, including varieties with deep purple leaves, such as 'Dark Opal'. A tender perennial, treated as an annual in cold climates, it grows to roughly 25cm (10in) tall. Basil is among the most aromatic of herbs, and each variety has a slightly different flavour. Enthusiasts often grow several forms. The most commonly grown (and usually found in supermarkets) is the Italian basil, 'Genovese', which is possibly the most aromatic; it makes excellent *pesto*.

purpose

Used as a flavouring for pasta and fish in particular.

cultivation

Sow seed in warmth in early spring and harden off outside when all danger of frost has passed. Site containers in full sun in a sheltered position and keep well watered. Snip off leaves as required. Remove any flowerheads.

marjoram
origanum majorana

This hardy perennial herb, also known as oregano, grows to about 30cm (12in) tall and has highly aromatic, small, dark green leaves. There are numerous cultivars with slightly different heights and habits, including the yellow-leaved form, 'Aureum', known as golden marjoram. Flowers are borne in early summer.

purpose

Excellent for flavouring soups, stews and egg dishes.

cultivation

Sow seeds in mid- to late spring and thin out to one plant to each 15cm (6in) pot. It is fairly drought tolerant, but prefers partial shade because the leaves of some cultivars will scorch in full sun.

parsley
petroselinum crispum

There are two principal types of parsley: curly-leaved, such as 'Moss Curled' and flat-leaved, such as 'Italian'. Flat-leaved parsley has a slightly stronger flavour. Both grow to around 23cm (9in) tall.

purpose

Parsley is a diuretic and helps to remove toxins from the body. Used in large quantities it can be dangerous, but in the amounts normally used in cooking it is perfectly safe. In culinary terms, it adds a fresh flavour to many oily or buttery dishes.

cultivation

Sow the seed in spring or summer. Parsley is notoriously slow to germinate (it can take six weeks), but the process can be sped up by soaking the seeds overnight in hot water. Sow thinly in a 15cm (6in) pot and thin out and transplant seedlings into other small pots once they are large enough to handle. Alternatively, grow it as an edging plant.

rosemary
rosmarinus officinalis

This is valuable half-hardy shrub for container growing. Plants can be trained into neat standards or clipped into geometric shapes, growing naturally to about 1.5m (5ft) tall. The highly aromatic leaves are needle-like and grey-green in colour, and pale blue flowers cover the uppermost shoots in early summer. There are many varieties, some lax and prostrate. The highly aromatic *R. officinalis* var. *angustissimus*, or Corsican rosemary, is tender but good for container growing.

purpose

Use rosemary to flavour lamb, chicken, fish and potato dishes in particular. Put a sprig on a barbecue or grill to scent the air as well as flavour the food. It improves circulation and aids memory, apparently.

cultivation

Rosemary grows very easily from summer cuttings and does best in alkaline conditions, so add a little lime to the standard compost mix. Grow it in full sun. It is splendidly drought tolerant. Clip it back in late summer to improve its frost resistance.

sage
salvia officinalis

This is another good half-hardy shrub for containers, particularly the purple-leaved variety known as 'Purpurascens', which has a wonderful purple-grey bloom to the leaves.

purpose

Use sage with offal, fish, eggs, cheese and beans and in stuffings for fatty meat, such as pork or duck, or oily fish, as it helps the digestion of fats.

cultivation

Grow sage from cuttings taken in early summer. Position containers in full sun. Clip back in late summer to early autumn.

thyme
thymus spp.

Another of the truly aromatic herbs, thyme, a hardy perennial, has a long culinary history dating back to the Greeks and Romans; it grows naturally around the Mediterranean. The tiny leaves can be either green or variegated in gold or silver. The plants make a low, spreading mound about 15cm (6in) tall. Bluish-purple flowers appear in midsummer.

purpose Thyme is good for aiding the digestion of fatty foods, such as pork or goose, and is excellent for stuffing poultry and other white meats. It is good, too, with cheese and eggs. Thyme is claimed to be a deterrent to flea beetle and cabbage pests.

cultivation

Grow from cuttings taken in summer. Position containers in full sun and use a layer of gravel as a mulch around the crowns of the plants, as they do not like to become waterlogged. Harvest the shoots in summer, after flowering, cutting roughly two-thirds from each stem. This will not only give you thyme for drying over winter but will encourage more bushiness in the plants.

BELOW (LEFT TO RIGHT)
A variegated sage (*Salvia officinalis* 'Tricolor') and thyme, of which there are many different varieties, is shown below.

EDIBLE FLOWERS

There are a number of flowers that can safely be eaten, some of them having medicinal properties, too. It is well worth growing a few edible flowers not only to decorate salads and other dishes, but also to introduce some colour into the planting. Most of them do not possess great flavour, but a few flowers or petals on a summer salad makes it look more decorative. Courgette flowers are delicious fried in light batter.

Some edible flowers are familiar, simply as the flowering element of an edible plant, such as chicory or courgette. Others are slightly unexpected; who would have thought that the somewhat virulently coloured day-lily was safe to eat? Flowers can also be candied as decoration for cakes and puddings, and individual flowers can be frozen into ice cubes for use in summer drinks and punches, or frozen into an ice bowl as an attractive container for a chilled or frozen dessert. To do this, fill a pudding bowl two-thirds-full with water, add the flowers and then place another slightly smaller bowl inside it, weighted down to stop it floating. Put the whole ensemble in the freezer for eight hours. When it is fully frozen, remove the inner bowl.

Don't overdo the use of flowers in salads; use just one or two as decoration. If possible, pck them just before you are ready to serve the dish. The flowers that follow are all suitable for growing in containers.

RIGHT Marigolds (*Calendula officinalis*) can be used to decorate salads; they are also a deterrent to whitefly.

borage
borago officinalis

This tough hardy annual with large, slightly hairy leaves has a rather untidy habit but startlingly beautiful cerulean-blue flowers. It grows to about 60cm (24in) tall. You can add borage flowers to summer drinks and cocktails. One unusual way to decorate drinks with borage is to freeze the individual flowers into ice cubes. Drop a flower into the water in each section of the tray before freezing it. (You can use other small edible flowers, too.)

cultivation

Sow seed in 15cm (6in) diameter pots and thin to two to three seedlings to each pot. Then allow the strongest to grow on. Alternatively, take root cuttings from an established plant in spring. Cut short sections of root, about 8cm (3in) long, and insert into a pot of compost and sharp sand, with the crown end uppermost. Borage prefers sun but will cope with partial shade. Keep it well watered.

pot marigold
calendula officinalis

A fast-growing annual, pot marigold grows to about 45cm (18in) tall, although there are dwarf varieties, too, such as 'Fiesta Gitana', which is much smaller. They have daisylike single or double flowerheads, composed of many tiny petals in bright orange, yellow, gold or cream, depending on the variety: 'Indian Prince' has dark orange flowers; 'Lemon Queen' has double lemon-coloured ones. They have a long flowering season, from midsummer through to autumn.

cultivation

Sow the seeds in small pots in spring or in autumn (put cloches over the pots if you live in a cold climate). Pinch out the leading shoots once the plants are a few inches tall to encourage them to bush out and more flowers to form on lateral shots.

courgette
cucurbita pepo

The bright yellow flowers of courgettes are edible, along with the attractive fruits (see pages 79–81 for cultivation information). Since the male flowers do not produce fruit, eating some of them while leaving enough for pollination purposes maximizes the usefulness of the plant.

nasturtium
tropaeolum majus

This vigorous annual climber has kidney-shaped, light green, large, slightly waxy leaves and exotic-looking, large, spurred flowers in red, orange or yellow, from summer through to autumn. The flowers (and their seeds) and the leaves are all edible, and the leaves are a rich source of vitamin C. The plants need support on a frame, wire netting or similar upright structure.

although there are small bush nasturtiums that require none, among them the Alaska series, which has variegated yellow-splashed leaves, and the very attractive 'Empress of India', which has slightly smaller than usual, purplish-green leaves and deep red flowers. It will normally make a clump about 25cm (10in) high and wide.

cultivation

Sow the seed in warmth in spring in small 15cm (6in) pots and transplant into larger pots after frosts are over. Alternatively, use them to edge other climbing vegetables. If you are short of space, plant them in hanging baskets. Keep them well watered.

Among the easiest container plants, pansies come in many forms, but the smaller flowered ones are probably the most attractive for decorating salads. You can find pansies that are winter flowering as well as spring- and summer-flowering forms. Most pansies grow to about 15cm (6in) in height, spreading to around 25cm (10in). They have a lax habit, making them a good choice for hanging baskets.

cultivation

Sow the seed of winter pansies in summer and of spring-flowering ones in late winter. Pansies need frequent watering, particularly when in flower.

pansy
viola spp.

BELOW (FROM LEFT TO RIGHT)
A courgette flower, nasturtium flowers and a pansy.

FOR THE LARDER

It just might happen that you have too many fruit or vegetables to eat immediately, in which case the most sensible thing you can do is to store them for later use, primarily by freezing them but also, for root vegetables and apples and pears, by storing them. Alternatively, turn vegetables into soup or pickles, and fruit into jams.

FREEZING

Some surplus vegetables can be successfully frozen. These include whole green beans, broad beans, peas, peppers and chillies. Tomatoes can be frozen if you puree them first. Vegetables that do not lend themselves to freezing can often be turned into soup, which freezes very successfully. Any fresh vegetables should be blanched before freezing. Plunge them into boiling water for a couple of minutes and then plunge them into cold water for the same length of time. Put the vegetables into a plastic freezer bag, suck out the air using a straw, and close and label the bag. To freeze soup, use airtight self-closing bags, pre-labelled.

STORING

Apples and pears can be kept for a while if they are laid out on a wooden rack in a cool, dry, dark place. Potatoes and other root vegetables keep best stored in a cool, dry place in a paper or hessian sack so that they do not sweat and rot. Hang under-ripe tomatoes and peppers in a cool, dry place, to ripen on the vine.

Many fruits can be made into good-quality jams. Some are less high in pectin (which helps them to set) than others. Those that lack pectin can either be combined with those that have more of it, or you can add lemon rind and juice, which will improve setting. Those fruits containing the most pectin are apples, blackcurrants, plums and gooseberries; those with medium setting ability are apricots, blackberries and raspberries; those with poor setting ability are strawberries and cherries.

The ratio of sugar to water is the key to setting ability, as is rapid boiling. Some fruit will set much more quickly than others. If the jam doesn't set as well as it should, keep it in the fridge, which will prevent mould from forming (a common feature in jam that has not set fully). When making jam, remember to sterilize the jars properly and be sure to allow the jars to cool completely before sealing them because any condensation will quickly turn to mould. You will get roughly 2kg (5lb) of jam for every 1.4kg (3lb) of sugar.

Making pickles and chutneys out of your own produce is very satisfying. The results make good presents as well, with the added cachet that you grew the ingredients, organically, yourself! Salt is the element that does the preserving, so do not eat too many pickles if you need to avoid salt for medical reasons.

JAMS

BELOW LEFT A glut of tomatoes can be used to make tomato sauce for pasta, which can then be frozen for later use.

BELOW RIGHT Raspberries can be frozen or used for jam.

PRESERVES

USEFUL RECIPES

green tomato chutney

450g (1lb) green tomatoes
1 sour apple
1 onion
75g (3oz) sultanas
2.5cm (1in) root ginger, grated
1 tsp salt
150ml ($^{1}/_{4}$pt) vinegar
50g (2oz) brown sugar

Skin the tomatoes, peel and core the apple, chop the onions. Mix together with grated ginger and the sultanas. Bring the vinegar, sugar and seasoning to the boil in a heavy-based saucepan. Add the ingredients and simmer until the mixture thickens. Pour into heated jars and sterilize in a moderate oven for 30 minutes. Allow to cool. Then seal.

mixed fruit jam

1kg (2lb) mixed fruit
1kg (2lb) granulated or preserving sugar
150ml ($^{1}/_{4}$pt) water

Top and tail the gooseberries and wash the other fruit, removing any stalks or hulls. Put all the fruit, sugar and water in the saucepan and heat slowly to dissolve the sugar and soften the fruit. Sterilize the jars by washing them thoroughly and then putting them in a low oven to dry out. Boil the jam on a fast boil for about 15–20 minutes until it sets. Test the jam every 5 minutes or so for setting by spooning a small amount onto a china saucer, allowing it to cool. If it wrinkles when you push it with the spoon, it is set sufficiently. Spoon the jam into the jars, allow it to cool, and then seal and label the jars.

vinaigrette dressing

6 tbs extra virgin olive oil
3 tbs wine vinegar
$^{1}/_{2}$ tsp strong mustard
pinch of sugar
seasoning

A good, basic vinaigrette dressing makes all the difference to any salad. Simply shake the ingredients up in a screw-top container. Use as much as you need and keep the rest in the refrigerator (it will last for a week or so). You can vary the dressing by using lemon instead of vinegar, or by using specially flavoured oils and vinegars. Walnut oil with raspberry wine vinegar is a winning combination. For a sweeter taste, use a little balsamic vinegar instead of normal wine vinegar.

basic soup recipe

Wash and peel the vegetables. Peel and chop the onion. Add the onion and garlic to a heavy-based saucepan and sweat in the oil for a few minutes. Add the vegetables and cook for a further few minutes, add the seasoning, stock and herbs. Simmer until the vegetables are just tender. Blend briefly and add cream or yoghourt, as required. Decorate with a few herbs. It is best not to serve soup piping hot or much of the flavour will be lost.

450g (1lb) chosen vegetables (eg potato and artichoke or leek)

1 onion

1 clove garlic, crushed

1 tbs olive oil

seasoning

750ml (1^{1}/4pt) stock

1 tbs fresh herbs, chopped

2 tbs cream or yoghourt

green herb sauce

If you do not want to go the bother of making a white sauce, try this one instead. It is excellent with fish or baked or boiled ham. The basis of it is Claire Macdonald of Macdonald's Cream and Chive Sauce.

Put the cream in the saucepan with the lemon juice and heat gently for a few minutes. Stir in the chopped herbs which will turn it a delicate green, add the seasoning, and serve warm with fish or chicken dishes.

425ml (^{3}/4pt) double cream

squeeze of lemon juice

3 tbs chives, parsley and rocket, chopped

seasoning to taste

organic growing media and fertilizers

The aim of organic gardening methods is to garden with nature, rather than against, so that you take as little as possible from the natural environment, and to replace what you do take. The following is a brief guide to some of the organic products you can buy or make yourself.

growing media

Look for growing media which are either peat-free or do not use freshly dug peat (bi-products of water filtration plants contain peat, for example) to prevent the further depletion of natural peat bogs. There are various substitutes, based on substances such as coir or brewer's spent grains, that can be employed as a base, although they will need supplementary fertilizers as they lack the fertilizing ingredients of natural peat. Organic gardening organizations usually provide their own recommended mixes. In addition to the usual range of readymade organic seed and potting composts, you can buy organic growbags.

If you want to make up your own growing medium, then make up a mix using 7 parts of clean loam to 3 parts of coir and 2 of coarse grit. Add 25g (1oz) garden lime and150g (6oz) blood, fish and bone meal) per bucketful of growing medium. A sowing mix can be made with 2 parts each loam and coir, and 1 part grit, with 50g (2oz) bone meal and 25g (1oz) garden lime per bucketful. The nutrient element in these growing media will usually last for four to six weeks; after that you will need to add your own nutrients. In addition to the usual range of readymade organic seed and potting composts, you can buy organic growbags.

drainage issues

If your growing medium is too heavy for certain purposes, for example raising seedlings, you can add grit or perlite to improve its drainage ability. In other cases, for example for hanging baskets which dry out rapidly, you can improve the moisture-retaining qualities of the growing medium by adding special seaweed meal moisture-retainer with the compost. It works in a similar way to non-organic moisture-retaining crystals.

fertilizers

There is a growing range of organic fertilizers, some general purpose and some formulated to provide appropriate feeds for plants with particular needs, such as to promote fruiting. The rates of application are normally indicated by the manufacturer, and should be adhered to. Adding extra for luck can result in problems!

Among the many different organic fertilizers at your disposal are those based on seaweed. For container gardening, liquid seaweed extract is ideal as it can be used either as soil improver or a foliar feed, and is quicker acting that seaweed meal which is normally mixed in with the growing medium. It contains natural plant growth stimulants and an extensive range of trace elements that help plants to take up the nutrients. Other good natural fertilizers are liquid feeds that are based on comfrey or farmyard manure.

General organic fertilizers for adding nitrogen and phosphates are generally made up from a mixture of bone meal, dried blood and farmyard manure.

glossary

annual Plant that completes its lifecycle in one season.

biennial Plant that completes its lifecycle in two years, growing in the first year, and flowering and fruiting in the second.

cloche Glass or plastic structure which protects plants, either from cold weather or from insect predations.

cordon Trained plant in which the growth is restricted to one leading stem; often used for fruit trees.

F1 hybrid Used to describe the first generation offspring of a cross between two genetically distinct parent plants.

half-hardy Used to describe a plant that can tolerate temperatures just below freezing for short periods only.

hardy Used to describe a plant that can tolerate temperatures below freezing for long periods.

hybrid Naturally occurring or artificially created offspring of two genetically different parent plants.

open pollination Pollination that occurs naturally in the wild.

peat Naturally ocurring, moisture-retentive, humus-rich organic matter, used for potting compost and derived from sedge peat or sphagnum peat. Peat substitutes, such as coir (coconut fibre), garden or mushroom compost, bark chippings, brewery grain residue and leaf mould are more environmentally friendly alternatives.

perennial Non-woody plant that lives for two or more growing seasons.

perlite Granules of minerals added to compost to improve aeration and/or drainage.

pH Measure of acidity or alkalinity. Most garden plants prefer netural to slightly acid conditions with a pH of between 5.5 and 7.

pinch out To remove leading shoots to encourage bushiness or to stop further growth.

potting compost Well-drained but moisture-retentive growing medium.

pruning Removal of surplus growth to improve shape of plant or to encourage flower/fruit production.

spur pruning A system of shortening the lateral shoots in order to stimulate flower or fruit bud production.

tender Used to describe a plant that cannot tolerate conditions below freezing.

suppliers

ORGANIZATIONS

The Henry Doubleday Research Association
Ryton Organic Gardens
Coventry
CV8 3LG
01247 6303517
email: enquiry@hdra.org.uk
Europe's largest organic membership association. Provides information and general assistance to members. Heritage seed library. Has three gardens, at Ryton, Yalding in Kent and Audley End in Essex, open to visitors.

The Soil Association
Bristol House
40–56 Victoria Street
Bristol BS1 6BY
Tel 01179 290661
Email: info@soilassociation.org. uk

SUPPLIERS

Chiltern Seeds
Bortree Stile
Ulverston, Cumbria
LA12 7PB
Tel 01229 581137
Suppliers of flowers, herbs and unusual varieties of vegetables.

Jekka's Herb Farm
Rose Cottage
Shellards Lane
Alverston, Bristol
Tel 01454 418878
Organic herb plants

Ken Muir
Dept TG12X
Honeypot Farm
Weeley Heath, Essex
C016 9BJ
Tel 01255 830181
Supplier of fruit including special dwarf varieties. Also publishes Grow Your Own Fruit *(£4.99), an excellent guide to fruit growing.*

The Organic Gardening Catalogue (in association with HDRA)
Riverdene Business Park
Molesey Road
Hersham, Surrey
KT12 4RG
01932 253666
email chaseorg@aol.com
Suppliers of a large range of seeds, organic products and books.

Suffolk Herbs
Monks Farm
Coggeshall Road
Kelvedon, Essex
CO5 9PG
Tel 01376 572456
Email: suffolkherbs@internet.com
Seeds of unusual vegetable varieties as well as herbs.

index

ACKNOWLEDGEMENTS

The author would like to thank the following: Steve Wooster for his superb photographs, Madeleine David for her captivating illustrations and Anne Wilson for her elegant design; John Wingate, chairman of Golders Green Allotment Association, for growing some of the vegetables and herbs in containers; the HDRA for the use of their library and Maggi Brown in particular for her helfpful comments on the text; Val Bradley and Carole Handslip for their useful comments and contributions; Corinne Asghar and Lydia Darbyshire for their editorial work; Marie Lorimer for the index; Ken Muir for information on fruit growing. Last, but not least, thanks to the late Frances Lincoln and her staff, in particular Anne Fraser, Jo Christian, Anne Askwith, Becky Clarke and Michael Brunström. Thanks, too, to Ginny Surtees, who commissioned this book.

PHOTOGRAPHY CREDITS

All photographs copyright © Steven Wooster except for the following, all copyright ©The Garden Picture Library: p 30 David Cavagnaro/GPL; p 31 Michael Howes/GPL; p 73 Philippe Bonduel/GPL; p 94 Friedrich Strauss/GPL; p 95 John Glover/GPL; p 109 Friedrich Strauss/GPL.